BRITAIN IN OLD PHOTOGRAPHS

HERNE BAY
REVISITED

JOHN HAWKINS

SUTTON PUBLISHING LIMITED

Sutton Publishing Limited
Phoenix Mill · Thrupp · Stroud
Gloucestershire · GL5 2BU

First published 1999

Copyright © John Hawkins, 1999

Title page photograph: Barges unloading on the
beach, early 1900s.

British Library Cataloguing in Publication Data
A catalogue record for this book is available from the
British Library.

ISBN 0-7509-2035-1

Typeset in 10/11 Bembo.
Typesetting and origination by
Sutton Publishing Limited.
Printed in Great Britain by
Redwood Books, Trowbridge, Wiltshire.

All photographs are a certificate of attendance

Roland Barthes
La Chambre Claire

CONTENTS

Introduction   5

1   The Seaside   7

2   The Seafront   19

3   The West Cliff   35

4   The East Cliff   45

5   Severe Weather   53

6   The Town   71

7   Special Events   89

8   People & Transport   101

9   The Surrounding District   117

     Acknowledgements   126

The Herne Bay Angling Association Challenge Shield. This fantastic silver trophy, which features views of the town and angling equipment worked in relief (*repoussé*), was first fished for in 1906. In the early 1900s the club's activities were recognised as being of importance to the town and this trophy was bought by public subscription at a cost of 100 guineas. The proud angler in this picture was one of the early recipients. The trophy is now permanently displayed at the club's headquarters just out of shot to the left of this picture. The Challenge Shield is still fished for and remains one of the club's most prestigious awards.

The drinking fountain in the background was presented to the town in 1888 by a Major Davies. When the seafront gardens were redesigned as part of sea defence works in 1993 this fountain was carefully taken apart, restored and installed at a new site in the Waltrop Gardens, along the seafront to the west.

INTRODUCTION

*H*erne Bay Revisited is the second selection of early photographs of Herne Bay compiled for this series of books. It is eight years since *Herne Bay in Old Photographs* was published, but people continue to ask questions about the streets and buildings shown in the pictures. Stories are remembered about some of the local characters who were long forgotten until glimpsed in a faded photograph. It is this continuing interest and enthusiasm that has encouraged the preparation of this second collection. As with the previous volume the selection of images for this book relies heavily on the output of local photographers, many of whom worked to produce picture postcards. Today these postcards remain an amazing source of early pictures, particularly from the years between 1900 and 1914 (the so-called 'golden years' of picture postcard collecting). This second book includes pictures from every decade of the twentieth century right up to the 1960s. The format chosen does not attempt to reflect the history of the town in chronological order; the selection of material used is essentially personal. Images that have been reproduced elsewhere in recent times have not been included: this decision means that some well-known events, such as the Pier Theatre fire in 1928, will not be found in this book as the pictures available are already well known. Where gaps occur in coverage, this may indicate either a shortage of material, the limitations of time and space or my decision not to use well-known pictures.

The town of Herne Bay has experienced two distinctive periods of growth separated by something of a depression. The first burst of activity was round 1800; the second was towards the end of the nineteenth century. In the 1790s people were beginning to consider the various benefits of sea bathing. An obvious place for the new bathing machines was the beach to the east of the Ship Inn. The Ship had been established here for many years, catering for the trade generated by the coastal trading vessels, or hoys, that used this part of the bay for collecting and landing their cargoes. Local trade must have been improved when visitors to the seaside started arriving on the old road from Canterbury. In turn the establishment of a military encampment on the East Cliff also attracted visitors and provided more local business. By the 1820s a small grid of streets was laid out off the road that ran back from the seafront inland to Herne and on to

Canterbury. This modest beginning was perhaps the first of the speculative developments by a landowner hoping to take advantage of the attractions of the seaside.

The London-based developers of the 1830s employed considerable artistic licence when preparing the engraved illustrations for their capital-raising prospectuses. A tradition of optimistically illustrating a concept rather than the reality has continued through a variety of grandiose local schemes right up to the late 1990s.

For contemporary images of this first phase of growth we must rely on drawings, prints and paintings. When considering the second surge of growth towards the end of the nineteenth century it is interesting to compare the following quotes. In a town guide of 1891 the introduction reads: 'a town that must shortly be well planned, well patronised and well out of its mysterious stagnation'. The equivalent passage in a 1927 guide reads: 'Few places are so favourably placed as this delightful holiday resort. Situated on the north coast of Kent, commanding extensive views of the open sea Herne Bay is indeed an ideal place either for residence or holiday.' The visitors' guide for 1960 describes Herne Bay as 'The Happy Resort'! This modest holiday town boasted a wonderful weather record: during 1958 Herne Bay was the UK top temperature resort thirty-six times, and in 1959 May, June, July and August recorded 1,057 hours of sunshine.

The development of practical photography happily coincides with the second phase of the town's growth. The local photographers Craik, Dickens, Pemberton, Palmer, Lowe, Scrivens, Simmons, Manners and others have, through their work, provided us with a window on the events, both ordinary and spectacular, that were part of life in the town during its progression from stagnation to delight. This selection includes pictures from the late 1890s through to the 1960s. Photographs of the town before the 1880s are not common; most that are known of have been published previously and are therefore not included in this book. Local history is essentially about people; Herne Bay has had its share of magnificent staged events and these are illustrated. Also included are scenes that somehow caught the photographer's eye but then perhaps got no further than a family album. All have some part to play in telling the story of the town's development.

I hope that as with *Herne Bay in Old Photographs* this publication may stimulate interest in similar material, and more people will come forward to put names to mystery faces. I hope that readers will continue to gain as much pleasure from looking at these pictures as I have in compiling this selection.

CHAPTER ONE

THE SEASIDE

F.G. Brown, the stationmaster, is seen here with two of the girls who worked in the buffet, late 1920s or early 1930s. At that time the stationmaster's house was adjacent to the station towards Fleetwood Avenue: the site is now part of a car park. Public transport, both road and rail, played a much more important part in people's lives before the widespread use of motor cars. Programmes for special shows and entertainment would offer late trains and buses, and on regatta or carnival days special trains were run to and from all stations to London.

Station Road, in a view looking towards the railway station from just past Spenser Road. As late as the 1920s the Grand Hotel on the left (see p. 78 bottom) was virtually the only building on the east side of Station Road between the railway station and Kings Road. A line of horse-drawn vehicles can be seen waiting for customers to arrive by train. This picture was published by Lowe & Co., whose premises can be seen next door to the Albany Bakery in Promenade Central (see p. 33 top).

The pier miniature trains were built and operated by Mr Liversage. These small-scale live steam locomotives were extremely popular with visitors to the pier in the years following the Second World War, when the full-size trams were no longer used. This particular engine was exhibited both at the Festival of Britain in London in 1951 and later at the Romney Hythe and Dymchurch Railway museum at New Romney. At his workshop in Kings Road Mr Liversage built model engines for wealthy collectors all over the world. In the 1970s, long past retirement age, he still drove around Herne Bay in a dark green Jaguar XK convertible.

This pier tram, which was built at Strode Park, carried huge batteries to supply motive power. After the start of the Second World War two breaks were cut through the pier to hamper enemy action. After 1945 the breaks were 'temporarily' bridged by timber rather than being repaired properly using steel. As this arrangement was never made good the trams were not able to run again. It is quite probable that the subsequent loss of structural integrity also contributed to the collapse of the pier in the gales of 1978.

In the very earliest town guides, published when visitors first started coming to Herne Bay, fishing was always sold as an attraction. The Herne Bay Angling Association was founded in 1903 and was a founder member of the National Federation of Sea Anglers (see p. 4). In the early twentieth century the London papers ran articles about the first tope catches of the season. The long pier provided anglers with the opportunity to reach fish away from the beaches without the need for a boat. This picture dates from 1909, and the rush bag hanging from the handle on the tram was of a type sold by the local tackle shop; they were often printed with the tackle shop's name and address, as in this example.

Fishing is the sort of activity that seems to attract as many spectators as participants, as can be seen in this picture taken from the pier head looking back towards the shore. At favoured times of the year it was not unusual for several hundred anglers to be using the pier at any one time. For big competitions the number would be even greater.

hese four girls sitting on a breakwater west of the pier are
oyly demonstrating the less than flattering nature of swimsuits
d hats made from cotton stockinette. From about 1870
athing costumes for men and women were remarkably
milar. Fashion, however, dictated that the ladies' styles were
change faster than men's: as the century progressed sleeves
ot shorter and the legs of the costumes became briefer. In
10 the Urban District Council bye-laws with respect to
ablic bathing ran to ten pages to explain some thirty-four
quirements: for example, stretches of beach were allocated to
agle or mixed sex bathing between scheduled hours. These
les were drawn up primarily for the use of bathing machines.
s people began to use the beaches as a place to spend time
ther than just for bathing from a machine so standards of dress
d behaviour changed, and it is not clear exactly how these
les were applied.

ilton Villas was a large semi-detached house in Station Road (in recent years it has been divided into flats) which was
ypical of the type of property that provided accommodation for so many of the town's visitors in the first decades of the
ventieth century. It was ideally placed en route from the railway station to the beach. The 1936 official town guide lists
9 hotels, 54 boarding houses and more than 80 addresses for apartments. Many photographs like this one show large
umbers of women and children with few men; it was not unusual for families to take some of their holiday without the
ather, who would be at work during the week and only visit his family at the seaside at the weekend.

A holiday under canvas was an economic way for many young people to enjoy a stay at the seaside. The local Boys Brigade often used a site north of the railway embankment and to the side of Canterbury Road, but while the embankment in this picture is almost certainly the railway these are not local boys. The camps were run on fairly military lines, and it is strange that the odd utensils and other bits of kit in the foreground were not tidied up before local photographer Fred Palmer from Tower Studios took this picture.

Hampton Hill had only a handful of houses built on it when this photograph was taken in 1912. The area was popular for camping with all sorts of youth organisations; some came to stay at sites that were already set out for them but these lads look as if they have a few hours' work to do before they will be ready for inspection. The importance of these camps to the town is demonstrated by the local paper. Throughout the summer season the front page was almost entirely taken up each week with reports of who was staying where and what they were doing.

Beach photographers produced thousands of pictures like these for people to take home as a reminder of their visit to the seaside. This one was taken in August 1923 on the beach opposite Promenade Central. Perhaps the family had timed their visit to enjoy the town carnival or regatta celebrations. The children all have the type of wooden spades which were sold for use on the beach but the buckets have a domestic look about them. The children's beach shoes, reminiscent of modern espadrilles, may well be home made.

This couple, photographed by Scrivens, are sitting on a boat just east of the pier. Although this photograph is probably about the same age as the picture above, it is worth remembering that it may be difficult to reliably date such pictures solely on the style of dress. For a variety of reasons such as social standing or affluence, not to mention personal preference, not all the subjects will be wearing the latest fashions.

The annual Carnival with its parade of floats and costumed entries has long had an important place in the town's calendar. In its modern form the parade is held on a Saturday, but when this picture was taken the parade was held on a Thursday – half-day closing in Herne Bay – an arrangement that enabled many of the town's shops and businesses to prepare their floats (see p. 99).

The pleasure boat *Blue Bird* ran trips from the beach below the East Cliff. This picture, taken at the top of the tide, clearly shows the use of the wheeled platforms that enabled passengers to board the craft in some comfort. This is not the same boat as the *Blue Bird* that was operated by Fred Palmer from in front of the clock tower in later years.

Opposite: This picture demonstrates that it was still possible to enjoy a picnic on the beach despite barbed wire and wartime restrictions. Back row, left to right: the man with the beaker is Tom Pitt, next to him is his son Mike, the little girl is Carol, the lady in the floral print is Myrtle Pitt (daughter of Charlie Fox who was a well-known local sportsman and landlord of the Victoria pub in the High Street), next to her are Joan Clark and Gracie. Front: the small girl in the hat is Diana, the boy is Kevin (known as Skipper). The limited access to the beach and restricted use of boats from 1939 to 1945 served in part to rest the inshore fishery. The immediate post-war years saw bumper catches, particularly of crab and lobster.

Riley's Revellers were a juvenile troupe providing a programme of entertainment that was advertised in 1912 as 'a mirthful medley of fun and frolic'. This picture was taken by Fred Palmer at Tower Studio. The troupe was usually to be found appearing to the west of the pier: this was not the most popular pitch as far as the artists were concerned (see p. 40).

Summer season entertainers on the sun deck at the Pier Pavilion (see p. 22). During the summer season Herne Bay boasted a huge range of entertainments. In August 1930 the *Daily Doings* lists Cabaret Follies at the Pier Pavilion (with a complete change of programme every other evening), *The Farmer's Wife*, 'a great comedy', at the King's Hall, the Argyll and Sutherland Highlanders Band at the Tower Gardens, and Punch and Judy on the Downs and at the East Cliff. The Bohemia (off Station Road) offered the Randell Jackson entertainers, while the New Casino Cinema was offering Janet Gaynor in *Four Devils* along with Douglas Fairbanks in the *Iron Mask*. For Regatta Week the Red Lantern Cinema in the High Street offered a 'Galaxy of Talkies'.

The RAF Cadet College Band played the 1927 season at the Central Bandstand from 28 August to 9 September. This was one of the twelve different bands that played on average fortnightly slots between April and September. Some of the young bandsmen that played the Central Bandstand during their National Service have since returned to play at Herne Bay, no longer in uniform but as part of one of the many enthusiastic civilian bands that are in considerable demand as the Services increasingly decide that their own bands are no longer economically viable.

Leslie Collins played the 1961 season at the Central Bandstand with shows at 3 pm. and 7.30 p.m. every day except Friday and Saturday afternoons. Dancing was offered at the King's Hall every Saturday, admission 4s. The Herne Bay Council entertainments manager Robert H. Fox had also programmed the show *Zip-A-Hoy* for the Pier Pavilion.

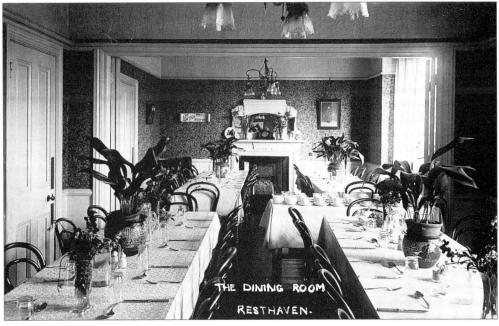

THE DINING ROOM
RESTHAVEN.

Resthaven was a Salvation Army Holiday Home for Women at the top end of Grand Drive. Although catering for larger numbers than most, this dining room was probably furnished and decorated in a very similar fashion to the many bed and breakfast establishments in the town.

Local boatmen were sometimes photographed in groups on the beach to provide picture postcard souvenirs of a day at the seaside. Quite why this group had their picture taken in the Shepherds Corner Studio we can only guess. Perhaps this is a family group of father and sons – many photographers used printed postcard stock photographic paper as a convenience, so a postcard back on a photograph does not necessarily mean that a picture had been produced to be sent through the post.

CHAPTER TWO

THE SEAFRONT

Herne Bay, early 1920s. This picture clearly shows the shape of the upper and lower bays dividing at a point just beyond the clock tower. The tide is at about half water and it is interesting to note how large the beach is between the pier and the clock tower – the accelerated loss of shingle caused by pushing the promenade seaward had yet to take effect. In the distance below Beltinge the bulge in the water line betrays a large landslip.

Herne Bay from the north-west, at least thirty years later than the view above. Many parts of the town are very different today. William Street car park can be seen as an area of grass known for many years as the athletic ground, and the nearby gas holder provided a considerable landmark in the centre of the town. To the west of the pier is the concrete tidal pool that was for some time home to the electric Glida boats (see p. 39 bottom). The beach itself clearly shows sand below the high-water mark; this was a feature of the West Beach until the 1970s. In the 1990s the annual August Festival children's sandcastle competitions made use of sand imported 7 tonnes at a time from Lydd, courtesy of the local company Bretts.

The Pier Theatre was constructed in 1884: the date can be seen picked out in ornate lettering above the central entrance. Facing the road there were a number of shops to each side of the entrance. In 1905 these included a fruiterer (Frederick Tarling), a tobacconist (A.J. Sutton), a chemist (Collen and Drayton), and a watchmaker and optician (E. Ellwood). Giovanni Mazzoleni ran a restaurant and the Herne Bay Pier Company Ltd had offices for their tram service. Various vehicles, including a couple of goat carts, can be seen, perhaps waiting to pick up steamer passengers and take them to their hotel or lodgings.

In the early 1900s the promenade east of the pier looked much as it had done when the formal gardens had been laid out to mark Queen Victoria's Jubilee in 1887. In this picture the promenade itself had just been extended beyond the second breakwater. The boxes at the top of the beach were used by the boatmen to store gear and fishing nets, and other equipment can be seen draped over the breakwaters. Between the second and third breakwaters there is an upright piano on a timber platform. By this time the alfresco beach entertainers who were capable of working with a minimum of props were beginning to lose out to more organised and commercial troupes – and this may well be a performer of the old school chancing his arm at what was certainly not a designated pitch.

The new Pier Pavilion was opened in 1910 (see. p. 91). The building was designed by the joint architects Percy J. Waldram of Charing Cross and Moscrop, Young and Glanfield of Bond Street. Constructed of timber on a steel frame, the building was complete with turrets, folding glazed screens and sun decks, ingredients that somehow capture the very nature of a fun-filled day at the seaside. The canvas screens blowing against the railings on the west side of the pier demonstrate one of the problems faced by anyone wanting to enjoy a deckchair in the sunshine. In later years staggered iron and glass screens were added through the centre of the wide neck between the shore and the pavilion; these glazed screens provided sheltered seating whichever way the wind blew. The screens also made the dash along the decking more bearable for spectators attending an event at the pavilion during the winter months.

The wide pier neck between the back of the theatre and the pavilion was sometimes used for entertainment as well as providing a good spot for stretching out in a deckchair. This picture clearly shows the metal frames that were used to support canvas windbreaks prior to the construction of the central staggered glazed screens.

Over the years the various businesses fronting the Pier Theatre changed hands: for example, by the mid-1920s the café was being run by P. Savoini. Dunsfords ran a lending library from the east side; they also sold all the usual seaside souvenirs and novelties. To the seaward end of the pavilion there was a diving platform built to accommodate the pier divers who provided live entertainment for the crowds at the appropriate state of tide, a tradition of such daring stunts that dated back to the late nineteenth century. In 1926 tickets for the Special Dance held at the Pier Pavilion from 8 p.m. to 11.30 p.m. cost 2s. The band of the Royal Artillery played daily at the Tower Gardens and the East Cliff, while there was a choice of variety entertainment at the Bohemia off Station Road and the chance to see Gloria Swanson in *Madame Sans Gêne* or Jackie Coogan in *Old Clothes* at the Casino Cinema.

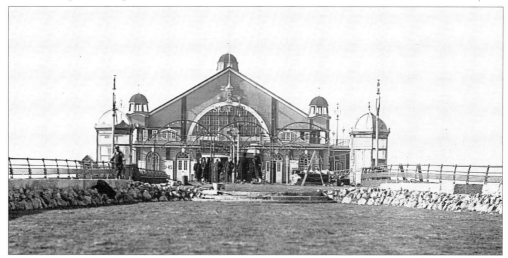

The Pier Theatre fell victim to one of the town's spectacular fires in 1928 (see *Herne Bay in Old Photographs*). The open vista left by the cleared site was greeted with delight by many people, as the theatre was by then nearly fifty years old and its facilities were lagging behind many more modern places of public entertainment. This picture shows the pier entrance in 1929; a garden and paths have been laid out as a temporary measure while the council deliberated over a number of grand schemes to redevelop the area.

The show *Poppies*, presented by Will Tissington and Katharine Craig, was enjoying its third resident season at the Pier Pavilion in 1934. The entertainments manager R.W. Davies Taylor (see p. 103 bottom) had to organise a full seven days of entertainment on the pier, military band concerts for Tower Gardens, a programme of music concerts at the Central Bandstand, and nightly plays and comedies at the King's Hall, as well as weekly competitions at both the East Cliff and West Beach bathing stations. If the local entertainment was not to your liking the New Medway Steam Packet Company was running a variety of trips from the pier head; for example, a round trip to Southend and Chatham by boat, returning from Chatham to Herne Bay by rail, cost 4s 4d.

The Pier Gardens provided a popular place for visitors to enjoy the sun and watch the world go by. After the loss of the Pier Theatre in 1928 there was considerable local pressure to keep this space open and maintain a vista that had not been available for almost fifty years (see p. 23). The sweeping curves and mock stonework seating and walls seen in this picture are typical of seaside architecture in the early 1930s; similar details could be seen in the extended building nearby on the site of the old rocket life-saving equipment store.

The Tower Gardens were looking a bit worn and sad by the 1930s. The gardens had originally been laid out using topsoil removed from King's Road when the schools were built. However, poor drainage, regular doses of sea water and windburn from the salt-laden onshore breezes all combined to give the gardeners a hard time. The popularity of this central part of the seafront also meant that there was considerable wear from the sheer weight of foot traffic. It was not until the redesigned gardens of the 1990s were completed with built-in automatic irrigation that the gardeners could be sure that all their carefully planned schemes would look good for the whole summer season.

It is interesting to compare this picture (which is about the same age as the bottom view on p. 20) with the similar view on p. 21. The most obvious change is in the size and height of the beach produced by the loss of material following the advance northward of the promenade and construction of the Central Bandstand. The interesting combination of ramp and steps in the foreground was designed to enable beach boats to be hauled up from the beach; this well-worn stone structure (which looked much older than it was) was demolished during the building of the sea defence scheme in 1992–3.

In the early twentieth century military bands played at the flagstaff between the pier and the clock tower. This photograph by Pemberton shows the 7th Dragoons, and the year is probably 1905. Bands were booked by the Herne Bay Military Band Committee, a group which held fund-raising events to pay for the bands and also recovered some income by letting out chairs to people listening to the music. Many of the pictures in this book are picture postcards which have messages on the reverse side; these sometimes provide intriguing details of a day at the seaside. Writing to a friend in Beckenham, the sender of this card had apparently walked to Hampton on the previous evening and enjoyed a bag of cherries bought in the town for 8*d* per lb. The card was written on the pier, which shook 'awful' when the tram went past.

The Central Bandstand interior, showing how the enclosure of the rear of the bandstand ensured protection for the audience from the wind in any quarter. Enclosure also provided the opportunity to collect an entrance charge, rather than the previous arrangement which relied on charging for the use of chairs. This picture also shows people sitting out in deckchairs on the sun roof; unfortunately modern regulations mean that this enjoyable feature will not be available to the public using the building in the new millennium.

By the early 1960s, when this picture was taken, most of the built ingredients of the seafront at the height of its popularity from the 1920s to the 1940s were still in place. However, for many people the idea of a holiday at home was beginning to pall; cheap air fares and holiday packages were soon to cause many traditional seaside resorts, such as Herne Bay, to decline rapidly – a trend that was not reversed until the 1990s. The comic story of such a failing resort (the fictional Gormleigh-on-Sea) and its attempts to rescue its fortunes was told in Ken Russell's first feature film, *French Dressing*. Somewhat ironically, the film was shot at Herne Bay within a few years of this picture being taken.

The promenade between the Central Bandstand and the clock tower is shown in this picture, which was taken as a publicity shot in 1960. The sloped apron at the front of the seawall was built to prevent the foot of the wall being undermined by waves sweeping away the shingle in rough weather.

The Dolphin Hotel advertised in 1910 that it was the town's oldest hotel, established in 1834. There had been a Dolphin Inn virtually on the beach until the construction of the first pier. The building in this picture was the result of negotiations that secured a top-class hotel on a site as near as possible to its predecessor.

The Central Café and Restaurant had succeeded the Tower Hotel in this prominent position on Tower Parade, one of the busiest stretches of the seafront. A crowd can be seen in front of the clock tower probably enjoying some alfresco entertainers working on the beach. In the distance horse-drawn brakes are lined up ready to take visitors on trips round the district. In the late 1920s the motor car had still to make its impression on the pace of the seafront.

Coastal trading had been carried on from this stretch of coastline long before people thought of visiting the seaside for pleasure. Hoys were used in early years for carrying both goods and passengers; in later years barges became the norm, particularly for bulky goods such as timber and coal. There were a number of landing points on the stretch from the west end of town (below what is now Albany Drive) east to the beach below the Ship Inn (which was the original landing point for the hoys). In this picture large cargoes of timber can be seen; when the tide dropped away horse-drawn carts were used to carry goods away to yards and depots in the town. In the middle distance a yacht running pleasure trips can be seen approaching what is now known as Neptune Jetty; beyond that is another yacht, probably working from the beach below the Ship. Although it looked picturesque on a warm summer's day, bringing these flat-bottomed barges right up to the beach had its own special hazards in unfavourable conditions (see pp. 56 and 57).

Small open beach boats, usually clinker-built, provided the opportunity for visitors to get afloat if they did not fancy a trip on one of the larger yachts. As well as oars, some carried small lug sails enabling them to take advantage of a favourable breeze. Boatmen, like the chap sitting on the breakwater, would take visitors out fishing as an alternative to a gentle row round the bay. Providing bait and tackle for fishing was a useful supplement to the boatmen's income in the summer months. The grassed area behind the promenade, which was used by some of the alfresco entertainers during the season, provided useful storage for these boats during bad weather.

Single-storey shops were built to the west side of Mr A.G. Iggulden's Promenade Central, taking up what had been the front gardens of St Augustine's Terrace. This picture shows how some of the businesses used their roof areas for seating. Herbert Boulding's off-licence at no. 9 and the Royal Devon Tea Rooms next door are now home to the headquarters of the Herne Bay Angling Association. This picture was published by Lowe & Co., whose premises can be seen in Promenade Central two doors along from Boulding's.

The new shelter shown here was listed under the heading 'Still More Improvements' in the official town guide for 1923–4 (along with the West Cliff shelter, see p. 43 top). Built from reinforced concrete with steel and plate glass screens, it was to provide seated accommodation for sixty people and standing room for a further two hundred; a ladies' retiring room was also incorporated. The building replaced an open grassed area previously used by entertainers in the summer and for storing beach boats in the winter months. The shelter was demolished in the 1970s.

The clock tower from the east. On the right-hand side of this picture it is easy to make out the granite setts forming a ramp down into the shingle where horse-drawn carts brought cargo from the barges up off the beach and on to the road (see p. 55). What is not so easy to make out is the registration number of the pale vehicle in the centre; it is D8251. Thanks to the work of David Bubier, we know a lot about this vehicle. Local businessman Frederick Wacher had started to run a passenger service from Herne Bay (his yard and starting point was just beyond the Divers Arms on the left of the picture) to Canterbury on 25 May 1912. This was a successful venture and he duly bought a second vehicle, D8251, a 30hp Lacre, which went into service on 25 July 1912. According to the clock tower the time is 10 o'clock, which means the vehicle had just started the second of its six daily round trips to the Rose Hotel at Canterbury.

The clock tower was built between 1836 and 1837 as a gift to the town by the slightly eccentric widow Mrs Ann Thwaytes. The tower originally stood practically on the back of the beach; successive promenades and sea walls have been built between the tower and the sea. This picture, taken in the early 1920s, shows the grassed area that was soon to have the new concrete shelter built on it, with the underground gents' toilet beyond. Motor vehicles are parked in the road next to the tower where a few years earlier there were lines of horse-drawn vehicles (see p. 28).

Charabanc outings were a popular treat with visitors to the town and the Tower Hotel and Restaurant was in an excellent position to capitalise on the trade. In the 1890s the then owner J.W. Collard not only organised such outings but also arranged entertainment at popular nearby destinations such as Reculver. To complete the package he also provided the catering for the trippers on their arrival. J. Dyke, the owner who followed Collard, continued this trade when he took over the business. The passengers in this picture all look as if they are going to enjoy themselves: the front vehicle has on-board entertainment with live music, and the man third from the back is pointing a camera back at our photographer, Fred Palmer. The maids looking out from the first-floor windows are perhaps wishing hard for their next day off.

The large holiday crowds of the early twentieth century were as much a target for an evangelical mission as they were for the itinerant tradesmen to be found along the seafront selling lemonade and ice cream. This group gathered together just east of the clock tower has the relative luxury of benches, which were perhaps carried down to the beach from one of the nearby chapels or church halls.

romenade Central went through several phases of development in the 1920s: the owner Archibald Iggulden was quick to
ick up on any new ideas that could be exploited to his advantage. In this photo the new entrance to the Winter Gardens
allroom has just replaced the Albany Bread Company (which has moved one shop to the right, reusing part of its earlier
rop fascia). The Winter Gardens was offering Fred Wildon's 1926 Margate Entertainers with reserved seats at 2s 4d. The
asino Pictures were showing Zane Grey's *The Thundering Herd*, starring Jack Holt and Lois Wilson.

he corner site where William Street meets the seafront had for many years been occupied by the single-storey post office
un by A.W.G. Philpott, who was trading there in the 1890s when Archibald Iggulden's site next door was still allotments.
y about 1909 Miss Margaret Bayly was trading there in 'Fancy Goods'; she was followed by Joseph Snelling who, as well
s selling seaside souvenirs, also ran a variety of tea and refreshment rooms from the adjoining properties between the
reet corner and what was then the National Provincial Bank. It was not until some years later that a business arrived that
vas to give the site its popular name, Macaris Corner (see p. 65).

Access to the beach was controlled during both world wars and photographs of military installations do not often turn up. This picture was taken by Fred Palmer. There is a note on the reverse written by W.R. Stanbrook of the *Herne Bay Press*: 'Herne Bay during the Great War, 1914–1918, barbed wire defences on the sea front, opposite the Tower Gardens west of the clock tower.'

On Saturday 6 April 1912 the Herne Bay Rink Hockey Club was host to Putney, then the International Champions. In front of a delighted crowd of 1,600 Herne Bay won the game 2–1. While the town slept the white elephant seen here was painted on the pavilion roof. The council was quick to clean off the offending words and picture but not before Mr Palmer of Tower Studios had taken this photograph. The use of the white elephant was taken to be aimed at non-rink hockey fans, who said that the proposed new pavilion would be a disastrous white elephant when the building scheme was first proposed to the council. Some eighty-one years after the incident local roller-hockey historian Roger Pout was able to name the mystery artists in his book on the early history of the game.

CHAPTER THREE

THE WEST CLIFF

Studd Hill Estate was laid out with all its roads named after makes of motor vehicles. The earliest holiday homes were tiny and often of relatively light-weight construction. The cliffs seen in this picture were quite unstable with frequent falls and slips. They were drained and regraded in the 1950s with a sea wall and promenade to prevent erosion at the back of the beach. The only substantial building in this picture is the row of coastguard houses in the middle distance. A brickworks chimney can be seen beyond: these distinctive landmarks were a familiar sight locally on the numerous brickfields that spread across the area west of Lane End and north of Sea Street.

West Cliff Drive is a grassy track in this picture that looks west across Hampton Pier Avenue. The small, somewhat lonely bungalow on the left is now much extended and surrounded by other properties. The buildings at the foot of the slope have not survived, while in the distance Studd Hill Estate is still in its infancy with only a scattering of chalets.

Wolseley Avenue was one of the main roads through the estate. Although the estate was growing fast there were still more gaps than buildings until the 1930s, and this picture also shows that the area rising up to the east beyond Hampton Pier Avenue was at this time still relatively undeveloped.

Susan's Shoppe was the only shop actually on the estate. Custom came not only from visitors using the new holiday chalets, but also from the large numbers of children staying at the holiday camps based in huts, which had developed from the earlier tented sites. New holiday sites were also being developed to the west at Swalecliffe; many of these visitors walked across the cliffs and came through to Herne Bay in search of entertainment.

Hernecliff Gardens at Hampton. This photograph shows the most seaward row of houses, the first to become part of 'disappearing' Hampton. Plots of land in this road were sold at auction in 1888 but this area was far from ideal for development, as it was generally low-lying with a small brook running through it and out to sea. In the great storm of 1897 waves ran straight through the end properties, and the situation was made worse by accelerated erosion of the protective beach following the completion of Hampton Pier. This picture, taken in 1905, looks across the brook from Hampton Pier Avenue: none of these houses was to survive another ten years.

Hampton Pier was built to serve the Herne Bay, Hampton and Reculver Oyster Fishery Company, which was incorporated following the grant of an act of parliament in their favour on 25 July 1864. The pier, which was completed in late 1866, was held responsible for the deposit of beach material to the east and considerable loss through tidal scour to the west. The growth of seaside resorts at this time had led to the development of numerous 'patent' systems designed to limit coastal erosion; one such, the Case System of Groyning, was tested on several sites at Herne Bay in the 1890s. The use of timber posts and bundles of faggots driven into the clay that can be seen in this picture shows a more pragmatic approach to retaining beach material. The remains of similar defences could still be seen below the Central Bandstand (see p. 63 top) as recently as the 1970s. The Hampton Inn on the right, which was formerly the Hampton Oyster Inn, is another legacy of the oyster company venture.

West Cliff Regatta. In more recent years swimming races have been held between timber booms suspended on empty oil drum floats: perhaps someone questioned the safety of this starting platform suspended on the east side of the old oyster company pier at Hampton. Herne Bay used to enjoy two regattas each year, the Town Regatta (see p. 98 top) held east of the pier, and the one at the West Cliff held east of Hampton Pier. In addition to rowing races for local boatmen there were novelty events on the water such as the duck hunt and the battle between the miller and sweep – involving a couple of local worthies fighting it out with large quantities of flour and soot. The West Cliff event always had a good range of beach races for children. In the 1990s the Festival Regattas recreated the opportunity for children to once again enjoy traditional beach races such as stone and spoon, sack race, and three-legged race; the popular greasy boom competition provided altogether more adult entertainment.

The boating lakes at Hampton had started life in the 1860s as oyster breeding ponds. In the early 1930s the landowner, developer Mr Ramuz, purchased electric boats from the Glida Boat Company of Canvey Island. One of their company engineers, Harry Chalk, came over from Essex to run the enterprise. Over a number of years the original ponds were extended, and the petrol boats seen in this photo (taken in the 1960s) replaced the early electric boats, which were moved to a concrete tidal pool just west of the pier (see p. 20 bottom). This pool was demolished as unsafe in the 1980s, and the site is now occupied by a rock groyne placed to limit the loss of imported beach material between the pier and Neptune's Arm.

The West Beach generally seems to have had a more relaxed feel when compared with the bathing station east of the Kings Hall. This picture shows the entertainers' site on the shingle (see p. 61), which was the lowest priced of the council's pitches – reflected in its earning capacity for the entertainers. Taken when the tide was low, this picture clearly shows how much the beach profile and composition has changed over the year; in the early 1920s much of the land beyond Lane End was still undeveloped. The changing tents on the beach in the distance were a warning signal to the bathing machines drawn up opposite St George's Baths, that bathing habits were changing – along with the ways that people used the beach.

Low tide on the West Beach. This picture is unusual in that it shows the beach at low water, allowing us to see how enormously long the early timber groynes were. This picture is slightly later than the one above. The tall timber poles fixed at the seaward ends were markers to help the pleasure boats to avoid the damage that could be caused by running over the groyne uprights when they were barely covered by the sea. I am delighted to be able to include a photograph that shows a bait digger at work.

St Georges Parade. In 1912 this row of buildings included the Kent Tavern, Wheeler's Oyster Saloon, Wilson's Tea Rooms, the Herne Bay College boathouse and St George's Tea Rooms. Compare this mirror-calm sea with the pictures on p. 59.

The beach west of the pier was home to the last of the beach entertainers; the enclosed seating area and small stage next to the pier approach introduced thousands of children to Punch and Judy each summer. Motor boats ran trips around the bay. The boat nearest to the pier on the west side was *Sea Spray*, built for Fred Palmer by R.J. Perkins of Whitstable. This was Fred's third pleasure boat; his first was the *Doreen* followed by *Bluebird*. Beyond *Sea Spray* the *Swordfish* can be seen. This was fastest of the beach boats, and the owner Bill Buck ran special trips out to the off-shore sea defence forts in this ex-naval rescue launch (see p. 15).

West Beach. This crowd on the beach below Bournemouth Drive seems to be enjoying some alfresco entertainment. The small bandstand seen at the foot of the cliff was removed to this site from the East Cliff in order to make way for the East Cliff Pavilion in 1903 (see p. 48 top). This beach was much quieter than those to the east of Lane End. In the early twentieth century many youth groups stayed at Herne Bay enjoying a cheap holiday under canvas (see p. 12), and the number of Boys Brigade uniforms in this shot perhaps shows that one of the more astute entertainers had decided to move west to pick up some custom beyond the usual established pitches.

When the promenade shown in this picture was extended west beyond Lane End it was necessary to demolish the coastguard station standing below Albany Drive. Away from many of the visitor attractions, the bathers on this beach were more likely to be locals or people staying in the town rather than day trippers. The public bathing bye-laws of 1910 designate this section of beach for male and female bathing from sunrise to sunset; Rule 25 stated that 'A person shall not bathe from any Bathing Place unless such person shall wear a suitable costume or dress (from the neck to the knee) to prevent indecent exposure of the person.'

The red shelter below Queensbridge Drive was built by the council in the early 1920s, reflecting the increasing popularity of the West Beach. It was listed in a 1924 guide to 'Healthy Herne Bay' under 'Still More Improvements' as offering seated accommodation for 42 persons and standing room for 175, with retiring rooms for both ladies and gentlemen. In this photo an almost continuous line of huts has replaced the changing tents of earlier years (see opposite), and it is interesting to note that the classic beach hut form with its steeply pitched roofs (see p. 63 bottom) so familiar today is not yet the norm. Sadly the terracotta dragon finials seen here on the shelter roof have long since disappeared. On idle summer days these fabulous creatures made wonderful targets for small boys; the damp clay from the cliffs behind provided ideal ammunition that not only stuck in place as proof of a perfect shot but also made a wonderfully satisfying noise on impact.

The West Cliff bathing station. Operated by C. Holness, this bathing station offered pleasant and safe sea bathing with expert attention, up-to-date cabins, diving stations and rafts. The Rendezvous café could provide trays for the beach, light lunches and dainty teas. If the sea was not to the customers' taste then at the baths across the road they could sample sea water or hot fresh water baths daily from 7.30 a.m. to 8 p.m.

Built between Selsea Avenue and Central Avenue, these substantial houses have superb views looking out across Western Esplanade to the sea. It is interesting to compare these houses with those in Canterbury Road (see p. 82 top). Almost all of the ornate details that add so much to the charm (and maintenance cost) of the earlier house have been pruned down to the minimum.

St Georges Terrace. Unlike many streets of large houses in the town, the owners of these substantial properties generally resisted the temptation to let rooms to visitors in the summer months. This picture shows the very neat streetscape created when front boundary walls are of a consistent style and size; it helps that at the time this photograph was taken there was no real requirement to create gaps for motor cars. The house on the corner shows curtains, timber venetian blinds (almost certainly painted green) and net curtains at the large sash window; some south-facing houses also had external blinds to screen the glass.

CHAPTER FOUR

THE EAST CLIFF

The maintenance of sea defences was a continuous challenge and drain on resources for the authorities. This striking photograph of pile-driving was taken by J. Pemberton in 1905 some 100 yards east of the Kings Hall. This part of the East Cliff is now associated with the Herne Bay Sailing Club (see p. 52 bottom); however, the timber building seen to the left beyond the drain vent pipe carries a name board for the Herne Bay Rowing Club – this helps to explain a number of early photographs of boats and crews taken at this end of the town. The short message on the back of the postcard reads: 'Soon be like Eastbourne now.'

This photograph from around 1900 shows the bathing machines belonging to W. Gipson: they are lined up ready to operate as the tide rises. In order to fulfil their function of providing discreet access to and from the sea these machines had to maintain their position relative to the water. At this bathing station the machines were moved up and down the beach with a series of large capstans mounted at the top of the beach. Demonstrating that some things never change, the small bare-footed boy appears to be throwing stones at the small girls dressed in their rather more formal promenading outfits.

Spray Cottage at the end of East Cliff Parade was the sort of pretty seaside property much loved by publishers of picture postcards. Unfortunately the high cost of regular maintenance has led to the disappearance of much of the detailed decorative joinery and ornate metalwork that made them so attractive. In the case of Spray Cottage the problems were aggravated by its very exposed position (see p. 58 top).

The Downs to the east of the town were very popular with the town's visitors. In this picture, which pre-dates the construction of the East Cliff Pavilion (see over), the undulating grass slopes provided a natural amphitheatre for a variety of entertainers. For many of the women in this picture the highlight of the day would have been to show off their holiday dresses. The bustles of the 1880s have disappeared but the plain skirt and hip-length jacket worn over a blouse are much in evidence; large elaborate sleeves have gone but necklines remain high. As the day got hotter ladies were able to remove their jackets, but gentlemen did not promenade in shirt sleeves; probably only the working class took off their jackets and sat down in shirts, waistcoats and hats. The timber-boarded flank wall of the end property of what was then East Cliff advertises George Rogers' Bathing Establishment, which offered hot and cold baths.

The East Cliff Pavilion was completed in 1903. This building replaced the earlier small bandstand which was removed and later repositioned at the back of the beach below Bournemouth Drive (see p. 42 top). Looking beyond the workmen who are completing the asphalt in front of the building, it is interesting to note the relationship between Reculver Towers in the distance and the headland of cliffs at Beltinge. The very different view today from the same spot clearly demonstrates how much land has been lost to the sea beyond Beltinge.

The Children's Special Service Mission was one of numerous evangelical organisations that worked with the crowds that were attracted to the seaside (see p. 32 bottom). The elaborate fashionable outfits seen in this picture were not Sunday best: this was an age of promenading when appearing in the latest style was an important part of the holiday experience. Certainly no one was looking to gain a suntan. Unusually, this picture shows a fabric windshield drawn around the bandstand on the pavilion roof; in later years glazed timber screens were added to achieve the same result.

Posted in September 1906, this postcard shows a sizeable crowd at the East Cliff Pavilion. The two young women in the foreground have blouses with extravagantly styled sleeves, although these had not been the height of fashion for some years. Many of the ladies have their hats perched precariously on padded bouffant hairstyles. With one exception, every child in the picture is wearing a hat or bonnet of some sort.

The new Kings Hall. The successful and popular East Cliff Pavilion was extended by the construction of a concert hall cut back into the cliff behind. This new building was opened by HRH Princess Henry of Battenburg in July 1913. The building was opened as the King Edward VII Memorial Hall, and the large posters seen in this picture demonstrate that it very quickly became known as the Kings Hall.

The Jollity Boys were one of the most popular groups of entertainers to appear at Herne Bay in the early twentieth century; they regularly secured the most profitable site on the East Cliff. The relatively simple stage in this picture was later replaced with their elaborate Fun Towers. Great care was taken when programming the season's entertainment to ensure that laughter from this site did not clash with the more serious business of a military band concert at the adjacent bandstand. When, as often happened, there was more than one band playing on the sea front, care was taken to avoid clashes of performance time. It was quite possible to walk the length of the front and not only to enjoy a bracing stroll but also take in a broad range of entertainment.

This crowd on the East Cliff opposite Beacon Road is probably enjoying a band concert at the East Cliff Pavilion prior to its extension to create the Kings Hall. In its early years the large building to the left operated as a private school for girls; later it became a hotel trading under various owners and changes of name. In 1936, trading as Hertford House, their advertising boasted 'the finest position in Herne Bay', and 'Central for all places of amusement'. Years later the building was divided into flats, and was finally demolished in the 1970s when the site was redeveloped.

The East Cliff bathing station was opened in June 1912. This picture was taken a couple of years later when attitudes to sea bathing were becoming more relaxed. However, the use of the changing cabins was still divided between men only (blue and white), women only (green and white), and family (red and white). In this picture the line above the crowd's heads was for drying out the costumes that were available for hire. It is quite likely that the crowd on the beach is watching a swimming demonstration by the man in the water: such instruction had for many years been part of the service offered by the bathing machine operators.

H 793   East Cliff from Downs, Herne Bay

The East Cliff seen from the Downs, late 1920s. This picture shows the bandstand on the pavilion roof in its final form, complete with glazed screens. One of the attractions of the seaside for many is that even on the hottest day there will be a slight breeze generated by the temperature difference between the land and the sea. This breeze was not popular with the bandsmen once it got strong enough to disturb their sheet music. Clothes pegs seem to be the most practical if inelegant solution to this problem. In the foreground a couple of girls fly kites: the gentle slopes and sea breezes were ideal for this particular activity.

Herne Bay Amateur Rowing Club. This is the only picture used in this collection which can also be found in my previous book *Herne Bay in Old Photographs*, I have included it in order to correct an error. I stated previously that I did not believe that such a trolley was the method used to get boats to distant regattas, but I was wrong. For many years the railway companies had made arrangements to carry boats and crews from one regatta to the next free of charge, often in a special train. When this concession was withdrawn the Herne Bay Club could not afford to pay 1s per mile per truck. Not wishing to drop out of the series, the club made up a boat carriage from a borrowed handcart and the boats were hand-propelled with the crews riding cycles. As can be imagined this led to some hairy moments on the road; on at least one occasion a boat ended up in a ditch. This sporting effort was recognised by the Mayor and Aldermen of Worthing who organised a public dinner 'In recognition of their plucky conduct in bicycling their galleys by road to the coast regattas'.

Herne Bay Sailing Club can trace its roots back to a meeting held in April 1921 when the Herne Bay Amateur Sailing Club was formed to promote the sport in the town. Races were started from near the Kings Hall. Most of the boats raced were 18 ft gaff-rigged Herne Bay Class boats. Essex One design and National 18s which were moored offshore lost favour over the years to more familiar modern classes such as Firefly, Heron, Hornet, Fireball, International 14, Albacore, Europe, Laser, Mirror and Topper. Over the years the club has successfully hosted World, National, Area and Open Championships. This photograph, taken in 1960, shows the beach between the club-house and the Kings Hall during Firefly week.

CHAPTER FIVE

SEVERE WEATHER

The storm of November 1897. This photograph was probably taken on Tuesday or Wednesday as the clearing up began following the storm of Monday 30 November. High winds from the north-west had driven waves past the sea defences and into the town. The central area north of the High Street between William Street and Richmond Street was largely under water; people in Market Street and Beach Street were rescued from their homes in small boats. Properties along the front were flooded as timbers torn from both the old pier and Hampton Pier battered through shop fronts and windows. In this picture the front windows of the post office run by A.W.G. Philpot, on the corner of William Street, have been boarded up. In order for repairs to be carried out to the damaged breastwork and promenades tons of shingle and smashed paving had to be removed by horse-drawn tip-carts. The one to the right of the picture is a fairly typical example of this versatile utility vehicle.

This bleak scene photographed at low water carries the title 'The dawn of 1905'. The picture was taken by J. Pemberton, perhaps from a first-floor window above his chemist shop at Oban House, 14 Promenade Central. The bleak winter scene with its fresh fall of snow is in total contrast to the animated scene on a hot summer's day, which is the way that so many visitors would remember this stretch of beach (see p. 29).

This photograph was also taken by J. Pemberton; the ramp was opposite his shop. High water on 1 December 1906 was at 18 minutes past noon. An hour earlier things had looked so bad that all the men employed by the council were summoned to work. The openings into Tower Gardens were closed with planks, and the dam shown in this picture was built across the slipway, consisting of timber planks pugged (sealed) with clay. These temporary barriers apparently held back large quantities of water. The merits of different forms of sea wall were generating much discussion locally with plenty of correspondence in the local paper at the time. This great storm with winds from the north-west lent additional interest to a public meeting that had been arranged for the following Wednesday evening at 8 p.m. The meeting had been called in order that the Chairman of the Council, Mr P.E. Iggulden, could present the authority's proposals for new sea-defence works.

The Barge *Caleb* was moored about 100 yards offshore when, in the small hours of 6 August 1908, a fierce sea driven by winds from the north-east tore away her ship's boat, the mizzen mast and part of her decks. As she was carrying 70 tons of kerbstones destined for Grand Drive she quickly settled on the bottom. The skipper, the mate and a labourer had climbed up the rigging to the cross-trees to escape the water; in this picture the Margate lifeboat has just picked up all three and is heading off to land them within the shelter of Whitstable Harbour. It had taken an hour for the lifeboat to sail to Herne Bay from Margate, no mean feat in these seas.

The barge *Thames* was driven ashore by gale-force winds on 12 January 1911. The lifeboat rescue of the three-man crew from the barge *Caleb* three years earlier led to two local men, Mr E. Renton and Mr E.J. Duveen, donating a rocket apparatus to the town for just such an emergency. (The building which housed the equipment can be seen to the east of the pier entrance in the picture at the top of p. 20.) In addition to the wreck of the barge, this January gale also brought with it the threat of flooding to the town. In this picture the waves can be seen running up the low ramped access to the beach (see p. 55).

This picture of the *Thames* shows the waves pounding her into the beach. Although unmarked, this is almost certainly a Pemberton photograph taken from the first floor of his premises opposite. The waves are flooding across the grass area in the foreground and the small beach boats, normally stored here in the winter, had probably been carried back across the road (see p. 58 bottom).

The wreckage in this picture is the remains of the barge *Star of Peace*. January 1908 had seen gales sweep across the country. On the morning of Thursday the 9th, the *Star of Peace* was laying off the front with a cargo of 100 tons of coal for the Herne Bay Gas Company. Owing to the gales her moorings had been strengthened, but there was an unusually high tide that morning, the moorings broke and the barge ran aground opposite the Albany Restaurant (see p. 33). The skipper's wife was safely brought ashore and attempts were made to unload some of the coal, the moorings were again strengthened and the barge floated on the rising tide. The situation was very precarious and made worse by the wind veering to the north-east. The moorings failed once again and she crashed down across the mouth of the culvert jetty below the clock tower. The barge was pounded by the sea but survived until early the next morning when, at about 5 a.m., she lost her mast. Dismasted, she quickly broke in half across the jetty, spilling cargo across the beach. This picture shows the crowds that gathered to watch the clearing-up operation at low water on Friday afternoon. As can be seen, the damage to the jetty was considerable.

Sea spray thrown up from the seawall provides amusement for small boys in this photograph taken by Pemberton in front of the Ship Inn, on what would appear to be a bright sunny day. The Ship itself had weathered many storms over the years; the scene was very different at this point in March 1906 when the ramp down to the beach (seen in this picture just beyond the lamppost) was completely smashed by the most severe gale experienced since 1897. (See *Herne Bay in Old Photographs*.)

When onshore winds and high tides came together shingle and flotsam from the beach would be carried across the road at a number of points. The piles of fishing gear stacked up against the garden wall on the left indicate that the blow had been forecast and that the boatmen had been able to move their equipment back to relative safety.

Many of the picture postcards produced showing fantastic stormy seas owed more to an artist's brush than gale-force winds. But this photograph, taken from the pier deck by Scrivens, shows the real thing and clearly demonstrates why the construction of a sea-defence breakwater arm was such a good idea.

High seas battering the front, 1948. This picture shows how the decorative low wall at the back of the promenade was of little use against waves, which were being thrown clean over the roof of the Central Bandstand.

'Whirlwind does damage at Herne Bay'. This was the newspaper headline in 1906 when on Saturday 17 November a new weather phenomenon visited Herne Bay. The day had apparently started fine with the wind rising by 11 a.m. with some light rain; by 1.30 p.m. the sky had turned black. The storm only lasted a few minutes, but in that time a trail of damage 100 yards wide extended from a point south-west of the railway station to the north-east for some 3 miles. Trees were shattered, sheds and fences were destroyed. This photograph shows some of the worst damage to property – a house in Glen Avenue at the Beltinge end of the trail of damage. These houses, at the time owned by Mr Hobbs, lost their roofs and were left twisted 'like a child's card house the instant before it falls to the ground'. The local paper used six photographs, all by Pemberton, to illustrate their story. In the next week's edition he was offering sets of the photographs for sale as picture postcards.

This picture and those on the opposite page show the result of a storm on 18 July 1924. The wreckage is from smashed beach boats and from St George's Baths, where Holness lost forty-two of his bathing cabins.

Gale-force winds had blown in from the north-west, and since this was the summer much damage was caused to equipment that during the winter months would have been safely stored away from the beach. One of the victims of the storm was the stage midway between the pier and the West Beach bathing station (see p. 40). This picture shows the torn remains of the tent covering. The figure nearest the camera is thought to be Freddie Fay: it was his concert party, the Frolics, that was performing that season. In the previous picture a wicker props basket with the initials FF can be seen smashed on the promenade.

In this picture the clearing up is still going on at the stage site. The message on the advertising billboard in the foreground reads 'Kent Messenger is out every Friday to give you the news & Freddie Fay's Frolics are out to amuse.' I suspect that 1924 was not a season that the entertainers remembered with much of a smile. A fund was set up locally as soon as the extent of the damage became apparent. Many local boatmen received financial help to replace boats and equipment from this fund, which attracted considerable public support. As this storm came at a time when the town's population was boosted by visitors, the fund did rather better than it might have done outside the holiday season.

The changing huts in front of St George's Baths appear to be performing a Mexican Wave following a summer storm. In the 1920s the proprietor C.N. Holness offered 'pleasant and safe bathing, with expert attention, up-to-date cabins, diving stages and rafts'. In the baths seen in the background hot sea and fresh water baths were available from 7.30 a.m. to 8 p.m. (Sundays 1 p.m.). This picture was taken by Percy Hargreaves of Parade Villas.

Severe storm damage is invariably measured against previous disasters. The impact of the storm of February 1938 which is shown in the next five pictures was compared to that of 1897, and was described as the worst in living memory. As had so often been the case in the past, gale-force winds from the north-west had caused huge seas to be driven across the seafront and past sea defences; torrential rain added to the misery making rescue work even more dangerous and uncomfortable. This picture looking west from the pier shows shingle and debris strewn across the road.

The new bandstand, which was opened in 1924, was designed by H. Kempton Dyson. A specialist in the field, he used this building to exploit the then relatively new construction techniques of reinforced concrete; Dyson later became a founder member of the Concrete Institute. This picture was used in the local paper to illustrate the damage to the 'east verandah', and clearly demonstrates how the sea was quite capable of severely testing any construction technique new or old. Restoration of the building in 1999 revealed that although some areas were well short of current thinking in terms of structural performance, other areas could easily exceed modern requirements.

The West Beach bathing station was one of the main casualties in this storm. By 1938 the site was no longer in private hands but was operated by the Council; private huts to the west fared no better. High winds had been blowing throughout the day on Saturday the 12th, and many people were concerned about what could happen with the evening high tide at 10.30 p.m. By 7 p.m., when waves were smashing into the balustrade at the pier entrance, the decision was taken to close the pier and the evening's skating was cancelled. This picture shows some of the crowds that came out on the Sunday, a bright sunny day, to inspect the damage. The boats in the foreground have been moved up off the beach and on to the grass slope of Lane End away from the waves.

These two pictures show some of the damage caused at the East Cliff. The gale also brought with it torrential rain and over 100 houses were flooded. Comparisons were made with the havoc caused in 1897. Although there had been earlier serious storms (see pp. 60 and 61) this one caused greater devastation simply because the town had grown so much since the 1890s. The East Cliff was particularly hard hit: twenty-four single and eleven double timber cabins disappeared completely. A relief fund was quickly set up started with cash still held from the 1924 fund. A pragmatic action was the Council's provision of a hundredweight of coal per flooded household: by the following weekend this offer had been taken up by sixty people. The total damage to public property was estimated at around £10,000, at a time when a return ticket to London cost 7s 2d and building plots could be bought in the town at £2 per foot of street frontage.

'reckage piled up at the foot of the grass slope just east of Lane End. This stretch of the seafront west of the pier had ıly a very low wall at the back of the beach (high seas were able to run right across the promenade), and during severe ɔrms the remains of beach huts and boats served as battering rams to smash the windows and doors of properties along e front. In the big storm of 1987, when the pier was finally destroyed, a resident of Marine Terrace was awoken by mething knocking on the French doors at the front of the house. She went back to sleep only to discover in the orning that the noise had been caused by a small boat hitting the doors, and a line of seaweed and debris showed where e waves had stopped only a few feet from the house.

he buildings on the seafront between William Street and Market Street were among those most likely to suffer whenever ıle-force winds and high tides coincided. Fifty-six years separate this scene from the picture on p. 54 but the problem is much ıe same, with a lot of clearing up to do. This picture was taken by Scrivens, and probably shows the scene on Sunday ıernoon following the storm that had raged through the small hours. Some of the broken windows have been boarded up ıd a fair number of people have braved the weather conditions in order to have a look at the storm damage. As in so many ırlier pictures in this book, some cannot resist staring straight back at the man with the camera. The storm of February 1953 ˙as the worst to hit the town since 1897. Nationally flood damage was reported along 1,000 miles of the east coast.

This picture of Mortimer Street and Beach Street was probably taken a little later but on the same day as the one opposite showing Culvert Passage. The flood water can be seen draining away left towards Richmond Street. In the great storm of 1953 the town had been flooded by the storm on Saturday night with high water at 2 a.m.. Conditions were such that although the water receded on Sunday morning further flooding occurred twelve hours later as the tide rose through Sunday morning. This picture was not taken in 1953, but shows flooding in either 1947 or 1949.

Mortimer Street between Beach Street and Richmond Street was always liable to flood. This is just about the lowest part of the town and either heavy rain or stormy seas – often combined – could quickly provide a watery view, in this case captured by Scrivens. There is a fire engine parked across the end of the road, and it is quite likely that the cellar of Scrivens' own premises on the corner of Richmond Street and the High Street was under water when this picture was taken.

Culvert Passage runs from Mortimer Street to the seafront between the backs of the properties in Market Street and Beach Street (see the picture opposite). As its name suggests, this alley follows the line of the brick drain built to carry Plenty Brook beneath the town. (The mouth of the culvert was below Lemonade Jetty, which can be seen on p. 27.) This alley is one of the lowest parts of the town and invariably suffered in even the slightest flood.

In this picture Mortimer Street is dry but water is still lying in the lower part of the alley, and at this stage the back yards and ground floors of the houses to either side in Market Street and Beach Street (north of Mortimer Street) would also have been under water.

Central Parade under water. This section of the front is relatively low-lying and was no stranger to flooding either from high tides and strong winds (see p. 59 bottom) or from torrential rain. The promenade between the pier and the clock tower ensured that this central section generally escaped serious damage from floating debris which was driven on to the more exposed sections – west of the pier and east of the clock tower – where there was no sea wall (see p. 65 top).

February 1956 was extremely cold. The last week of January had seen 11 degrees of frost recorded at Herne Bay, and the London forecast office received 15,488 enquiries through January. On the evening of 1 February the temperature record on the Air Ministry roof was the lowest for nine years. These two pictures, taken by Scrivens on 2 February, were used on the front page of the *Herne Bay Press* to illustrate the headline 'Plumbers up to their necks'. The report said that on Sunday the 5th more than 500,000 gallons of water were wasted in Herne Bay, much of this water being pumped out through burst pipes. The mast and rigging shown in the lower picture are on Hampton Pier, and the ice gives a pretty good indication of where the wind had been coming from. Later that year, in March, it was reported that the sea froze for some 100 yards.

The winter of 1963 saw Herne Bay in the grip of what were described as arctic conditions. Snow had started to fall in Kent on Boxing Day 1962; in some places this was not to clear until March. The *Herne Bay Press* of 18 January reported that the sea froze on Saturday night, and the temperature had dropped to minus 6.3 degrees centigrade (10 degrees of frost). Ice had begun to build up near the pier and quickly extended along 3 miles of the sea front. On Monday ice flocs several feet thick littered the beach. This picture taken at Hampton shows some of the hundreds of visitors that came to see Herne Bay's ice show. By the time this picture was taken in the second week of the freeze, the pack-ice stretched out to sea for approximately 1½ miles along the whole of the north Kent coast.

As the ice was swept past the town on the ebbing tide, Scrivens captured this amazing picture, taken from the pier deck just inside the second shelter. Ice floes can be seen disappearing into the distance. It was reported that at one stage the ice stretched out for 3 miles. In the foreground neat lines have been cut where the ice is being swept past the pier legs.

The *Herne Bay Press* of 8 February reported that the sea had been frozen since 13 January. Coastal shipping had been warned to watch for an extensive floe some 2 miles long off the Kent coast. This picture of the pier pavilion shows how crusts of ice built up on the beach as successive tides rose and fell each day.

After a fall of snow the evenly grassed slope of the Downs on the East Cliff provides an excellent site for tobogganing; only the dress style (particularly the ladies' hats) and lack of plastic sledges separates this crowd photographed in 1909 from their modern equivalent.

CHAPTER SIX

THE TOWN

This unusual view of William Street shows Gordon House, the double-fronted baker's shop of T.B. Clark to the left; next door and occupying the corner site is Hogbin Brothers Ltd (auctioneers, house furnishers, agents and removal contractors – telephone number 2). On the next corner is the studio of Shepherd's, the photographer that produced this picture. The advertising sign on their front wall is offering twelve postcard-size prints for 1s.

Herne Bay head post office is an imposing High Street building, which carries the date 1907 above its central door. In 1910 the Postmaster Mr W.A. Ashmore was managing opening hours that would raise eyebrows today: weekdays (including Saturdays) 8 a.m. to 8 p.m., Sundays 8.30 a.m. to 10 a.m. The telegraph service was available at both the High Street and Avenue Road, and the town boasted six branch offices and twenty-one pillar boxes. There were seven dispatches of mail to London, and four local deliveries of letters on weekdays with one on Sundays. This building later became home to the public library: much of the research for this book was carried out behind the window seen between the doors in the centre of the picture.

Mortimer Street looking east, before the days of the motor car. In 1905 the Kent Coast Stores was run by Fred Wood; between his shop and the Rose Inn on the corner of Little Charles Street there was a restaurant, a fruiterer, a watchmaker, a draper, a sweet shop, an estate agent (Wilbee and Sons) and a butcher. Ninety-four years later all these trades, apart from the butcher, are still represented in the same row, although not necessarily at the same addresses. Beyond Little Charles Street the Congregational Schools occupy a site that was redeveloped as a parade of shops in the 1930s. The large 'Stores' sign beyond is on the wall of A. Gandy and Co., grocers and wine merchants.

The High Street looking west from Dolphin Street. The first shop on the left is the fried fish shop of R. Read: these premises have remained variously a chip shop and/or a wet-fish shop for the last sixty years. Next to Read's is the Central Dining Rooms. In this picture the last house in the row before Cowell's is a private house, which was extended in the late 1920s to become the premises of J.W. Eve, family butchers. Cowell's was a traditional grocer, which offered a free delivery service to account customers right up until the early 1960s.

Ralph Libby, photographer of 20 Mortimer Street, took a series of pictures of the Central Supply Stores, 53 William Street, sometime in the early 1900s. This interior view of the shop is one of those pictures and was reproduced in a *Mates Town Guide* of 1902. The advert describes their own celebrated scotch whisky at 3s 6d per bottle: economic stability was such at this time that five years later they were still offering scotch at the same price. The business had been established in 1845 and by the time this picture was taken they were the largest family grocer and provision merchant in the town. Although the shop

has been specially stocked for this picture the range of goods usually offered was considerable. Among the company names that are familiar today are Ind Coope brewers, Stone's ginger wine, Mackeson & Co. ales, Schweppes minerals, Guinness stout, and Huntley & Palmer biscuits. In addition to the familiar names there are baskets of fresh eggs, hams hanging from the ceiling, stone jars of preserves and rolled ox tongues. Cabinets, glass-fronted cases and baskets hide much more. What a selection! And there was a man in an apron to serve customers as well.

No. 102 High Street had been a confectioner or baker for many years prior to the arrival of M. & G. Christofides. In 1932, when W.E. Hudson had this shop, Herne Bay boasted at least sixteen independent bakers serving a population of 11,872. The 1999 population of 35,000 would require forty-seven bakers to meet the same ratio, but excluding the supermarkets there are in fact only a handful left in business.

Avenue Road had a very rural feel in about 1907. The barrow on the left is typical of the sort that was used to carry visitors' luggage to and from the station or pier to their lodgings (see p. 21 top). The short length of fence and gate behind the two figures on the left probably marks the back entrance to Herne Bay College in St Georges Terrace (see p. 41 top).

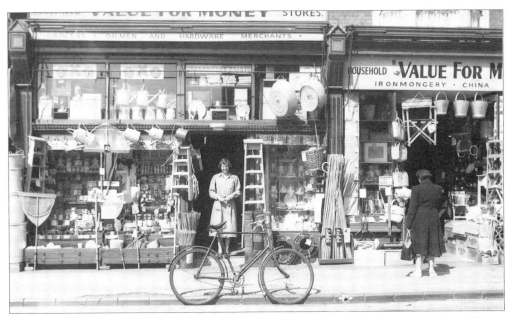

The Value for Money Stores at the High Street end of Station Road stocked a huge range of goods for use around the home. They were also ideally placed for visitors arriving by train who would pass by on their way to the seafront. This picture was taken in July 1953: the left-hand window includes a patriotic display featuring the Queen's portrait. A price tag tells us that 10s 6d would buy the biggest shrimp net they had on offer.

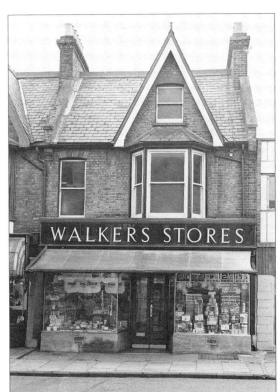

Walker's Stores at 36 High Street probably had this picture taken by Scrivens for publicity purposes. It shows their Christmas window stacked out with boxes of crackers. This shop was typical of many small-to-medium premises that disappeared through the early 1960s as they failed to hold their own against the rapid growth of the new supermarket chains.

The Connaught Hotel on the seafront opposite
the Central Bandstand was opened in the 1890s by
G.H. Boncey. This was an important business in the
town and many local clubs and organisations used it
their headquarters. Here the building is decorated fo
the Royal visit in 1913.

The Coronation in May 1937 was marked in all sorts of different ways. In Herne Bay the Chamber of Commerce organised a window-dressing competition: a total of eighty businesses entered in two classes, with separate competitions for private houses and a special category for the best electrically lit premises. The judging was carried out by Councillor S.W. Pearce JP of Margate and Mr L.E. Martin of Ramsgate. The Creameries Ltd of 176 Mortimer Street seen here were the winners of Section A. They just missed winning the *Daily Mail* Cup, which went to Lanes Lending Library.

Opposite: The Grand Hotel had always been able to boast certain advantages in its advertising. It stood in its own grounds, and at the time of this photograph it was practically the only building on the east side of Station Road between the railway station and St John's Church. In 1927 it claimed to be the most modern and best-appointed hotel in the town and offered special terms for golfers. However, by the late 1920s it was having to offer 10 per cent off the tariff for the winter months and by 1936 (although still claiming to be renowned for its excellent and generous cooking) it was only open for the summer season. With improved communications and greater car ownership, Herne Bay was increasingly attracting day visitors, a shift which was directly reflected in the fortunes of the town's hotels.

These four pictures show various different boarding establishments. The Imperial was in Parade Villas, which was between Richmond Street and Sea View Square. After the downturn in staying visitors following the increased popularity of the motor car many of the B & B establishments reverted to private homes; some struggled on with lettings but by the 1970s most had been converted to private flats or were let as furnished rooms.

Another property in Parade Villas between Richmond Street and Sea View Square, 1913. The first three properties to the east of the Connaught Hotel (see p. 78) were run by a Mrs Howe: she is the lady standing in the gateway. The property is most probably decorated for the royal visit of Princess Henry of Battenberg in July.

The boarding house Abbotsford could be found in Canterbury Road between William Street and Charles Street. Salisbury House to the right was also a lodging house, and between this block and Charles Street was Sea View House, which in the early years of the century was run as a girls' school by Miss Watson. The three houses later became known as Ivydene: this too was run as a boarding house and was one of the larger such concerns in the town. Contemporary town guides list large numbers of hotels, boarding houses, apartments and so on; very few quote their rates, but many offer 'modest terms' and others 'reasonable rates'. I suspect that competition was such that a lot of adjustment went on through the season to accommodate changes in demand from week to week.

The Hebron Holiday Home on the south side of Brunswick Square was originally two houses. By the 1930s it had expanded into a third property and was advertised in the local town guide as a Home of Rest, with staff who included a Matron, Mrs Jacob and a Principal, Miss E.C. Thompson.

These large houses built on the east side of Canterbury Road just north of the Beltinge Road junction show many of the ornate details characteristic of their period; the use of elaborate timber detailing was to become more pronounced with the slightly later seaside villas. The qualities of much of the town's late nineteenth- and early twentieth-century residential building stock was a major part of the decision to create an extended Herne Bay Conservation Area in 1991. Over the years much of this richness has been lost. The ornate iron fencing was a casualty of wartime scrap drives.

Camden Villas were the only buildings listed on the west side of Selsea Avenue between Sea Street and Western Esplanade in the 1910 directory. By 1925 nine more houses or bungalows had been built: this picture dates from the 1920s. Such gradual development has contributed to the rich mix of house styles that can now be found right across the West Cliff – west of Lane End and between Western Esplanade and Sea Street.

John Street in the early 1900s was the section of today's Pier Avenue that runs between Central Parade (then St George's Parade) and Western Avenue (then King's Road). The bungalow on the left is on the corner of Clarence Street and was for many years known as Clarence Bungalow. In 1910 seven of the terrace of fourteen houses in this picture were listed as lodging houses.

The south end of William Street is not often found in early photographs. This picture was actually taken by Bells Photo Co. of Leigh-on-Sea, Essex. It is unusual to find a picture postcard of this date produced outside the town as Herne Bay had an abundance of prolific photographers of its own. Just to the right of the picture was the yard which was home to Cooper's Studio: the artist William Sidney Cooper was the great-nephew of the well-known artist Thomas Sidney Cooper. William had moved to Herne Bay in the 1890s and lived at 18 William Street, the first property south of the parish church and school room.

The houses on the right of this picture were built as Western Terrace. Up until about 1912 their address was Kings Road Avenue, which ran from Station Road to Albany Drive; this section then became known as Western Avenue. Much of the area between here and the railway station was developed in the 1920s and '30s by the local firm of Goodwin and Russel. They produced a catalogue of house types titled 'The Little Homesteads of Herne Bay'. In the distance beyond the horse-drawn cart we can see through to the backs of the houses in Minster Drive.

The shop on the corner of Station Road and Brunswick Square had been a butcher's for many years before becoming a dairy. Trading as Slade's Dairy, it was run by J. Bedford. The terrace on the right included the Hebron Holiday Home (see p. 81). Considering Brunswick Square's position off the main route between the railway station and the sea, it is surprising that more of the houses did not offer accommodation.

Mickleburgh Hill and Tyndale Park are both roads that were developed with large houses. In general appearance they are typical of many of the roads at the east end of the town. Although the houses are not as decorative as those shown on p. 82 both roads show the visual impact created by the consistent use of low brick walls topped with cast-iron railings and iron gates hung from brick piers. In some cases these walls and railings, along with other correct period details, are being replaced with the aid of Council grants.

The Catholic church in Clarence Road was dedicated by Fr Vincent Grogan CP on Wednesday 25 June 1890. The site had been part of a residential property, including walled gardens and stables, which was purchased in 1899 for £3,600. The purchase by the Passionists was made possible by the generosity of a wealthy benefactor, Mr Denis Broderick. As soon as the first community took up residence (May 1889) the Catholic congregation began to grow. By the time of the Coronation in 1902 the church was crowded to hear a loyal sermon from Fr Cuthbert Dunne CP.

The original chapel built on this William Street site in 1835 was purchased by the Revd Henry Geary, the Rector of Swalecliffe, for £5,300 in 1839. The parish church of Herne Bay was consecrated on 13 October 1840. The North Room to the left had been added in 1836, the South Room in 1839; both were the gift of Mrs Ann Thwaytes. This picture dates from the late 1930s; access to the parish church was much improved when this elevation was replanned in 1974. The modernisation and improvements to this building were made possible by the sale of St John's Church in Brunswick Square.

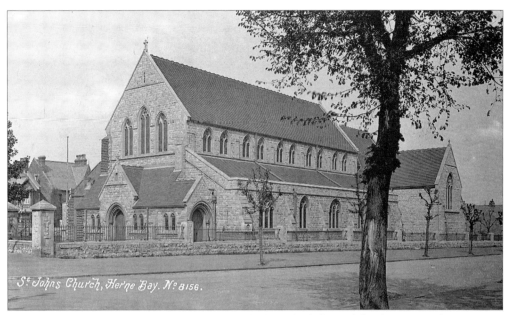

St John's Church in Brunswick Square had been built on land donated for the purpose by Sir Henry Oxenden, and was constructed by the local builder A.S. Ingleton. The foundation stone was laid by the Lord Mayor of London on Thursday 28 July 1898. The Order of Service for this ceremony was illustrated with a drawing showing the church with a square bell tower at the north-west corner. This tower was never built, and the toothed brickwork that can be seen in this picture remained waiting to be completed until the building was demolished in 1973.

'The Wooden Church on the Hill' was how many people knew St Bartholemew's Church. This elm-clad church was erected in only six weeks in 1908 by Messrs Boulton and Paul (the company that had supplied the shelters in the Tower Gardens built to mark Queen Victoria's Jubilee). This picture was taken by Fred Palmer on All Saints' Day 1913, and shows a crowd gathered to witness the laying of the foundation stone of the replacement building: this stone was built into brickwork that was to form a part of the west wall of the new church. On 30 July 1932 St Bartholomew's was consecrated by Archbishop Lang.

This signal box interior may be nothing to do with Herne Bay. Unlike the works picture below the photographer is not identified. Herne Bay certainly had a signal box, but is this one too big? The picture is included here as it was found amongst a lot of other local material. I look forward to a reader getting in touch and explaining just where it is.

This workshop could be almost anywhere. The only clue we have is that the picture was taken by local photographer Fred Palmer. It is included as it is typical of the sort of places where some of the people that appear in this book worked. The engine in the background that drove all these machines is surrounded by guard rails. Health and Safety legislation has moved on considerably in the last sixty years, and it is difficult to imagine quite what this space was like when everything was running flat out with all the unprotected drive belts and shafts busily thrashing round.

CHAPTER SEVEN

SPECIAL EVENTS

Sir John Knill, the Lord Mayor of London, came to Herne Bay on 3 August 1910 to open the new Pier Pavilion accompanied by the Lady Mayoress and Sheriffs, and the mayors of many Kentish boroughs. Days like this were important opportunities for the town, and the council and local businessmen went to considerable trouble and expense to ensure that Herne Bay was seen at its best, not only for the benefit of the invited guests but also for the visitors who were attracted to the event and, in particular, for people who might invest in the rapidly developing town. The photograph above shows part of the procession of thirteen carriages that had left the railway station soon after 12.30 p.m. The carriage on the right is the state coach of Sheriff Roll followed by the coach of Sheriff Slazenger; the Lord Mayor was next in the state coach pulled by four greys. This section of the High Street is built up on brick vaults: the fall to the natural ground level below can be seen behind the hoarding on the left-hand side of the picture. The decorated shops seen on the north side belonged to Mr Page, and the tall building in the centre was built as a shopping arcade (running through to Mortimer Street), and later became the Red Lantern Cinema.

Opposite: The official pavilion opening was performed by the Lord Mayor who was handed a key with which he opened the doors into the vestibule. Members of the Council and the Reception Committee (this event had involved a huge number of committees) were then presented to the Lord Mayor. A public luncheon followed with toasts, responses and speeches took up the remainder of the afternoon. The local paper quoted these at length in the following week's edition; the report included the response to 'The Press' which was made by Mr W.R. Stanbrook, editor of the *Herne Bay Press*. This picture shows Sir John Knill leaving the pier to return to London on the 4.12 train. The streets leading back to the station were once again lined with people. The day was rounded off with a band concert, dancing and entertainment. The Jollity Boys performed from the first shelter on the neck of the pier, huge quantities of confetti were thrown about and the entire day was generally hailed as a huge success.

he pavilion opening ceremony was conducted from what was then known as the pier extension. This was 44 ft wide and
0 ft long, and the new building took up some 96 ft of this – leaving a wide area of deck in front of the entrance and behind
e back of the original theatre. Chairs were set out to accommodate the visiting dignitaries and guests, and this picture
ows the various mayors and their ladies taking their seats in the front row. Canterbury, Chatham, Margate, Lambeth,
llingham, Woolwich and Gravesend were amongst those represented. The band of the 2nd Northumberland Fusiliers was
sitioned to the east side. In his speech the Lord Mayor remarked that he hoped this latest addition to the town would help
ract the London boats to call. No doubt many of the local businessmen heartily endorsed this view.

High Street, 1909. These four pictures show scenes from one of the town's most eagerly awaited sporting events. Held in May of each year, Godden's Derby was a series of walking races around the town with distances varying for different classes. The top event of the day was the Championship walk over 12 miles. This shows one of the difficulties faced by officials: as the races progressed the crowd tended to spread on to the road, which led to problems for the cyclists used by some of the walkers as coaches or pacers.

This series of races carried the name of W. Godden, who was the sponsor of the trophy for the main event, and was the proprietor of the butcher's shop Little Smithfield, at 22 High Street (which can be seen in the picture opposite). This photograph shows some of the race officials in 1912: the figure in the light suit is W. 'Daddy' Godden; the tall man third from the left could be Jimmy White (see p. 94 and p. 108). At the Smoking Concert held in the evening following the races, the prizes were presented and the various people that organised the event were thanked. On these occasions Godden frequently stated that he would like the day to be known as the Herne Bay Derby.

Godden's Derby, 1912 – tenth anniversary year. This picture shows the four starters in the Championship walk: W. Rose, F. Hart, W. Hudson and P. Disque. Rose is the shorter man on the left standing next to Mr Godden himself. Rose went on to win in 1 hour 51 minutes 15 seconds (3 minutes slower than the previous year's winner, A. Ells, who had apparently over-trained and could not race on doctor's orders. In 1910 Rose had won the cup outright for three successive wins (see *Herne Bay in Old Photographs*).

The Ladies' Handicap, which followed the main race, 1912. The lady in the foreground is probably Mrs Harnden, a favourite with the crowd, who was sixty-six years old and given a 12 minute start for the 3 mile race. The winner off scratch (no handicap) was Miss N. Dallaway in a time of 43 minutes.

The *Herne Bay Press* always joined in when local shops and businesses had the opportunity to put up decorations for a special occasion. This photograph, taken by Fred Palmer, almost certainly shows the newspaper's premises in July 1907. The special occasion was the visit to Herne Bay of Princess Louise, Duchess of Argyle, who came to the town to open an extension to the Passmore Edwards Railway Men's Convalescent Home at Blacksole. The building to the right of the press offices was the Star Drapery Company – milliners and dressmakers: they were agents for Dr Jaeger's Wool Clothing.

This burnt-out shop was Kemp's, the drapers in the High Street, opposite the fire station, which was run by Mr Kemp and his three sisters who travelled over from Whitstable each day. The shop had been locked up as usual on the Saturday night but the fire had taken a good hold before smoke was seen pouring from the roof on Sunday afternoon, 28 February 1909. There was heavy snow that weekend and it is possible that there were fewer people out and about than was usual. The fire brigade was summoned and the engine was run out across the road, but pressure at the hydrants was not good as some pipes may have been frozen. Despite the weather, a large crowd gathered to watch the spectacular fire which was not brought under control until early Monday morning. These are the sad remains of the shop later in the week; the figure not in uniform in the centre is fireman Lt J.S. (Jimmy) White, who had attended the fire at the weekend.

The Town Hall on the corner of William Street and the High Street was destroyed by fire on 12 June 1925. Herne Bay suffered from a number of major building fires through the 1920s: most of these have been well illustrated in previous books (see *Herne Bay in Old Photographs*), and are for that reason not included in this collection. This Fred Palmer picture shows the brigade fighting the fire from the west side: with the fire station just round the corner they did not have far to travel. This was a serious fire; the flames spread east through the council offices destroying some records and on to the fire station itself.

Promenade Central ablaze: the third major fire to occur in Herne Bay, September 1928. The whole building (see p. 33 top) was destroyed in the conflagration, which burned for four hours before being brought under control. The new Casino cinema that replaced part of the building can be seen on p. 65.

Empire Day 1917 was celebrated at Herne Bay with a service at the flagstaff in the Tower Gardens on Sunday afternoon, 27 May. This picture shows a detachment of D (Herne Bay) Company, 2nd Battalion Kent Volunteer Regiment being inspected by Lt-Col. S.C. Peters prior to marching down to the flagstaff. The service was later cut short by thunder clouds, large drops of rain and the threat of a severe storm.

The Peace and Victory celebrations of 19 July 1919 are shown in the next three pictures; similar scenes were repeated in towns up and down the country. The principal event of the day was the parade and march past of those who had served in the war. In this photograph the band of the 3rd Battalion Worcester Regiment head off along the front. Behind them in white caps and aprons are the VAD nurses led by Miss Campbell, acting commandant; the figures in white smocks are Land Girls, followed by the mounted figure of Capt. Lloyd, the chief marshal. Behind him is the banner of the Herne Bay branch of the National Federation of the Discharged and Demobilised Sailors and Soldiers: this was carried by representatives of the Navy and Army.

The civic party and dignitaries assembled for the salute at the bandstand built around the flagstaff. Virtually all the Council members were present including the Chairman, Mr N. Rowden junior, and the Vice-Chairman, Mr H.W. Hall. Lt-Col. Lang Sims OBE was in overall charge (see p. 112). The row of men standing in front of the platform with the white covers on their caps are the Army and Navy veterans.

The head of the parade that the group above were waiting for. The newspaper reports the following week quoted all the speeches at length and also remarked on the size of the crowds: the Tower Gardens were described as 'seeming to be one solid mass of people, and with the waving flags above, and the summer costumes of the ladies, the purple banner of the Federation [see picture opposite], the helmets of the fireman glistening like gold in the midst of blue and green, the scene was a most picturesque one'.

Regatta Day, 18 August 1921. This view of the pier deck shows Herne Bay enjoying what was reported as the best attended regatta in the town's history. The large crowds came in by railway and road; many from Canterbury made use of the vehicles of the East Kent Road Car Company. The promenade and pier were decked out with bunting, and the crowds were able to watch what was going on from rows of deckchairs along the promenade, which were all occupied early. This regatta was the first occasion when the Herne Bay Sailing Club joined the event with a special race; there was also the novelty of a balloon race launched from the Pavilion promenade roof. In 1921 the starting gun was a twelve-bore shotgun and the official starter can be seen holding it to the left of the picture. The organising committee list reads like a *Who's Who* of local businesses, council members and officials.

This fireman's arch was built across Central Parade in May 1935 as part of the Grand Pageant of the Empire, an event which was part of the town's celebration of the King and Queen's Silver Jubilee. At the front of the parade are the local platoon of 'A' Company 4th Battalion The Buffs, East Kent Regiment, with their drum and bugle band. The truck just passing under the arch carried Britannia (Miss Beryl Pearman, Miss Herne Bay 1935), who had a mounted escort provided by Mr Douglas' Riding School at Eddington. The parade started in Spenser Road and the route took in Canterbury Road, the seafront, Station Road, Kings Road and finished at the Memorial Park.

Carnival entries were variously decorative, amusing and just plain strange. This picture of the Wesley Players looks like a fairly typical Carnival Parade tableau, but the date for their performance at the Methodist Schoolrooms does not really fit with an event traditionally held in August. It may be that this float was made up to take part in the Coronation celebrations of 1937. The picture was taken by Scrivens: on the day following the August Carnival the High Street window of his studio would be crammed with hundreds of photographs showing floats and shots of the crowd. These were eagerly scanned by people looking for a record of their part in what was an important day in the town's calendar.

This giant tope was Frank Mount & Sons' entry in the 1929 Carnival. It was photographed outside their premises at the top of Grand Drive. The length of the tail may have given the parade organisers something to think about at some of the corners on the route. For many people original ideas such as this one were what the carnival parade was all about. Each year local clubs and businesses would try to come up with an entry that was better than their previous one. According to a poster in the *Daily Doings* the programme for the day on 22 August was as follows: 'Regatta at 1 p.m., Carnival at 6.45 p.m., Fireworks at 9 p.m., Carnival Dance 8.30–12.30. Bed at 1 a.m. (or it should be).'

On Monday 11 November 1918 the air raid sirens sounded, church bells rang, and crowds walked the streets celebrating the end of the war. This picture shows a group of soldiers who had been given leave to celebrate the peace by walking through the town. They made banners from flags, some draped themselves with the national colours and one carried aloft a disc painted with the red dragon of Wales. Drums and bugles were played – but this was not the usual military march, rather an infectious celebration of peace. Fireworks exploded and rockets shot into the air. Small children joined in, shops closed early and flags flew from every available point. The fine drizzle turned to rain, but even as dusk fell people seemed loath to return to their homes.

The scene at the flagstaff on the occasion of the presentation of the Meritorious Medal to ex-Sgt W. Hammant, 21 July 1925. He had served for twenty-one years in the Grenadier Guards and lived at Herne. Mr G. Cursons MBE, JP can be seen addressing the large crowd that had come to watch. In the background is the band of the 3rd Battalion, The Buffs. The actual presentation was made by the Chairman of the Urban District Council, Mr G. Blaiklock JP. The man wearing the boater and writing in his notebook is W.R. Stanbrook of the *Herne Bay Press*.

CHAPTER EIGHT

PEOPLE & TRANSPORT

Why is this crowd gathered outside the council offices? The rosettes suggest an election; however, in the early 1900s they were also worn to identify officials at events (see p. 93). We are pretty sure that the shortish figure with the large moustache and bowler hat standing sideways-on to the camera is Percy Edwin Iggulden.

On 31 January 1912 W.J. Flower and his wife both retired from the King's Road School. He had given forty-two years of service to the town, having started work in the boys' school in William Street in June 1870 as the only teacher of fifty-two scholars. By the time of the amalgamation of the boys' and girls' schools in 1880, Mr Flower was the headmaster. We know the names of some of the staff in the picture, which was taken to mark the joint retirement. In the back row the lady on the right is Ethel Eastland. In the middle row the bald man with the beard is Mr Flower, while on his left in the mortar board is Mr Hodginson. On Flower's right is his wife: she could boast thirty-five years of teaching service.

This picture, taken on the pier by local photographer E. Simmons, poses a number of tricky questions. For instance, it is not obvious exactly where on the pier it was taken. Several people in the picture are holding some sort of printed sheet. Was this perhaps a programme? Are they Pier Theatre staff with some of the artists from a show? The machines in the background are typical of the type that were lined up to either side of the pier entrance (see pp. 21 and 23). They variously offer 'chocolate', 'sweet preserved fruit and biscuit' and 'Sweet Treats'. Their substantial and ornate cast-iron cabinets were designed to stand outdoors, unlike the later more lightweight arcade machines.

The annual outing for the Pier and Entertainments staff, 6 October 1934. This photograph was taken as they got ready to leave the pier entrance. A number of councillors accompanied the staff. They took lunch at Anertons Hotel, Fleet Street, some then went off to watch Spurs play Leicester while others went to Kempton Park, and the day was rounded off with a visit to the Holborn Empire. Some of the staff names are known. Sitting cross-legged at the front is Dick Wilding; directly behind him, the man without a hat is R.W. Davies Taylor (the Entertainments Manager); behind him in the bowler hat is Titch Henley. The left-hand seated figure wearing a cap is Frank Holness, while the seated figure on the right is Mr Phippard.

On Tuesday evening 21 March 1905 the people of Herne Bay were treated to a glimpse of the future. Mr Arthur Thom.
Greenwood of the Central Supply Stores, William Street, had worked with Mr E.A. Mackenzie of London to bring a 2(
hp Thornycroft motor-bus to the town. On Wednesday a trial run to Canterbury had been arranged for members of th
Urban District Council, the Chamber of Commerce, the press and representatives of other interests. The importance of
reliable motor-bus link between the coast and Canterbury could not be underestimated. The test runs (there was a secon
trip for ladies in the afternoon) were a great success. The novelty of the vehicle was such that people came out of the
houses or stopped their work to stare as the deep blue and yellow monster passed by. This photograph was taken b
Pemberton minutes before the vehicle left and was on sale as a picture postcard by the time the party arrived back aft
taking their lunch in Canterbury. On the following Saturday the *Herne Bay Press* produced a special supplemer
describing the proposals for the vehicle. The list of applicants for share capital in the venture opened on 4 April. At th
time many towns were looking at experimental motor-bus services, but a novelty of the Herne Bay scheme was
proposal to offer at reasonable fares return tickets that would be available for return at any date.

Opposite: Fred Iggulden Ltd traded from these High Street premises as the 'Complete House Furnishers'. The Iggulde
family was once associated with so many aspects of life in Herne Bay that the town was sometimes referred to as Iggulde
Bay. The billboard and poster on the right of the picture are advertising another Iggulden business, the Auction Mart
128 High Street. This picture was taken by a young David Manners, trading from Bank Street, and shows the van fleet
the furniture business. The showroom building ran through from the High Street to William Street. The north er
incorporated the much earlier chapel building, which had given its name to the street opposite that ran down towar
Charles Street and the sea. All this area was cleared to build the Co-op supermarket.

.C. Mann traded as a coal, corn, flour and seed merchant from premises at 5 Sea Street, between Albany Drive and
andown Drive. These premises stayed more or less in the same line of business until the 1960s. This photograph was
ken in Cobblers Bridge Road where Mann had his coal stores. The houses in the background were known as Station
state at the time this picture was taken.

The passenger in this wonderful vehicle is Dr Tom Bowes MA, MD, BC Cantab, MRCSEng, LRCPLd. He lived a
Marine Terrace and his surgery was at the rear in Charles Street where this photograph was taken. The driver may we
be Walter Harris who later went on to run a garage from the premises in nearby Little Charles Street. It is interesting t
compare this imposing but fairly primitive vehicle with the neat horse-drawn trap opposite: the car representing th
latest thing in a new field of untested technology (and crudely over engineered in many areas); the trap a finely tune
sophisticated design incorporating lessons learned from years of refining style and materials to achieve function.
efficiency.

This very smart outfit was the sports car of its day, with every component at its optimum size to produce a lightweight vehicle. The card was posted from Herne Bay in 1905 with the cryptic message on the reverse 'But wait till you see the "missus!"'

Local boys as well as visitors to the town enjoyed outings by motor bus. This photograph was taken in Underdown Road in front of what is now the church hall built at the rear of the parish church. The window framed by a surround of two-colour brickwork can now be seen inside the hall. The picture dates from the late 1920s and may well show an outing for the choir or another church group.

In October 1908 the fire brigade of Herne Bay played host to the Deputy Mayor of Lyons, M. Gorjus. He was in Engla
as a delegate to the Congress on Moral Education but visited Herne Bay following a visit of the town's firemen to an eve
organised by the French Federation of Fire Brigades. This formal portrait was taken outside the front entrance to the Rc
Pier Hotel opposite the pier entrance. Back row, left to right: Cllr William Ruffell, engineer Charles Welby, Cllr Jo
Wilson, Lt James White, -?-, John Mackett, Capt. Frederick Wacher, -?-, Cllr Thomas Morris, foreman Alfred Inglet
Front row: -?-, -?-, Cllr Herbert Ramsey, -?-, Cllr P.E. Iggulden, Charles Levy, chief officer of Rochester and chairman
the South East Division of the National Fire Brigade Union, -?-, Cllr Edwyn Gedye, -?-, -?-, -?-. The local paper descri
M. Gorjus as having 'more the appearance of a Britisher than a Frenchman, tall and bearded with a frank open face an
genial manner'. In the morning the party had travelled by horse-drawn landaus, but their return journey was made
electric car.

Opposite: Scouts in Herne Bay celebrated their fifty-year jubilee in 1957. Following Robert Baden Powell's experimen
camp on Brownsea Island in 1907, the idea of scouting had spread quickly with troops forming all over the country. T
1st Herne Bay troop was probably one of the earliest to be started in north-east Kent, and its leader was Mr Norman Mil
who had been running a boys' guild in connection with the Congregational Church for some years. The guild beca
more popular once it took up the new scouting ideals. This picture was taken by Fred Palmer but we do not know if th
are local boys, as this part of the town was frequently used for camping (see p. 12). Apart from the early uniforms, one
the more interesting things about this picture is the large building in the distance. This is the Grand Hotel in Station Rc
(see p. 78): the camp is just north of the railway embankment, and the whole of the area between Canterbury Road and
railway station is almost completely undeveloped.

cal Boy Scouts were involved in the finale of the town's Silver Jubilee celebrations in May 1935. Across the country ey were responsible for lighting a chain of beacons. At Herne Bay this involved a torchlight procession starting at the ings Hall and heading for The Lees and Cliff Avenue; here the Chairman of the Council lit the beacon at 9.45 p.m. The e was chosen as it was as near as possible to the site that had given its name to Beacon Hill and Beacon Avenue. The seat own, which was presented to the council to mark the occasion, can now be found practically at the edge of the graded ff. In 1935 the bonfire was built well to the sea side of this position on what was then a broad area of grassed cliff top ee p. 98 bottom).

Members of the Herne Bay Division St John Ambulance Brigade were photographed, in 1926, against the background of the fence on the east side of the Herne Bay Athletic Ground William Street. The parish church can be seen in the background. We know almost all the names. Back row, left to right: Boswell, Gough, Cossey, Joy, Bartholemew, -?- Crouch, Honey, Clarke. Middle row: Spencely, Billy Smeed (of Smeed's Smart Signs fame), Beeteson (Council solicitor Cllr Cursons (Chairman of the Council), -?-, Dr Evans, Creasey, Keeler, Venn. Front row: Greenland, Avery. Mr E.H Gough (in the back row) had a son, Harold, who helped inspire an interest in local history that led to this collection of photographs being brought together.

This picture of members of the First Aid Party (FAP) was taken by Scrivens on the seafront just east of the pier in 1942. The FAP were based at the ambulance station in New Street and we know of four vehicles (including this one) that were commandeered for use by this group. Each vehicle was adapted in some way, either to carry equipment on the roof (stretchers in this picture) or on special trailers. Members of this group were among the first to report for duty at Canterbury following the bombing of June 1942.

The Herne Bay Entertainers were a local voluntary entertainment company that visited military establishments all over the area. This picture shows them alongside the East Kent bus that they used for transport, and the poster in the bus window is advertising one of their 1944 productions – 'Front Line Frolics'. Back row, left to right: Jose Warner, Pauline Wooten, Elsie Bed, Dorothy Wass, Ethel Le Galliene (pianist), Lil Heaton, Joan Joy and Rosemary Charlton. Front row: Alf Hill, Mrs Wheels, Alec Carnell (producer), Jo Sandercock (organiser), Pearl Lane, Margot Cooke and Horace Baines.

When Peace Day was celebrated on 19 July 1919 the salute was taken from a platform at the flagstaff by Lt-Col J.H. Lang Sims OBE, on the right. The man in the straw boater is Councillor W.J. Drew. The policeman is Sgt Byerley, one of two sergeants on duty that day.

On 4 September 1919 local Boy Scouts and Wolf Cubs took over part of the Herne Bay Lawn Tennis ground for displays, sales of work, competitions and games. The event was honoured by a visit of Aleck Tassell, Chief Scouts Commissioner. In this picture he is seen taking a great interest in an obstacle race (the boys are making knots). Behind the boys is the Vicar, the Revd C.E. Stocks; the other man, in the boater, is William R. Stanbrook of the *Herne Bay Press*, without whose work the text in this volume would be considerably shorter. A large number of the photographs in this book carry notes on the reverse that refer to 'W.R.S.', and he can be found in a great many of the pictures once you start looking for the man with the notebook.

This picture was taken by Pemberton in the early 1900s, and it is included as a reminder of the importance of farming around Herne Bay in the early years of the century. The town has never supported much in the way of manufacturing industries. Apart from employment deriving directly from what would in modern times be called the leisure and tourism business, one of the biggest employers in the area was agriculture. This photograph may have been taken at an event such as a ploughing match or perhaps a point-to-point race meeting. Whatever the event, the speaker, standing up on the wagon, is taking the opportunity to address the assembled farmers and their workers.

'The All Steel Bicycle' was an advertising slogan used by the manufacturers Raleigh for many years. This, photographed taken at the corner of Gosfield Road and Kings Road (then Kings Road East), is an extended bicycle that was almost certainly built by Curling and Lukehurst Cycle Engineers. It was probably created as a promotion exercise and it may well have appeared in the popular summer carnival. A number of local businesses were producing their own cycles as late as the 1940s; a small workshop in the White Horse Yard even produced bespoke racers that competed all over Europe. In the 1890s Root and Clarke had patented their own particular form of cycle tube joints and promoted their business with involvement in cycle racing.

In 1921 Dorothy Crouch was the winner of the decorated hoop competition (hers is the hoop on the left). This picture by Percy Hargreaves shows some of the contestants, and some of the entrants in the fancy-dress competition. The picture was probably taken on the East Cliff behind the Kings Hall.

These costumed children were photographed in front of the Pier Pavilion by Percy Hargreaves; the postmark on the reverse is 24 August 1920, and the message on the reverse refers to the children as prize winners. In 1920 the Annual Regatta and Carnival was not held until 2 September. It would appear that rather than carnival entries these children are more likely to have attended one of the Juvenile Fancy Dress Fêtes, run by the entertainer Will Evans and held at the Pier Pavilion each Wednesday.

Groups of workmen do not often get featured in this type of collection except on completion of a public building (see p. 48) or when employed doing something out of the ordinary (see p. 46). The first of these two pictures shows an excavation at Coopers Hill, between Charles Street and the seafront. The amount of timbering to the side of the excavation would seem to indicate that they are working at a considerable depth. Various people have suggested that this was a gas board job but there is no real evidence to support this idea. The photograph was taken by Scrivens.

These two fitters may well not be local men: as specialist tradesmen they may have worked for a company from some way away. The card was sent from Will to Jim in Hornsey Rise, London: 'Hows this rather swanky . . . please send my caiters [sic] down as soon as possible get trousers muddy on cliff.' The postmark is 2 November 1909. It is easy to forget that many of the buildings pictured throughout this collection are virtually brand new: in this example the brickwork joints are finished with tuck pointing, a technique which gives a very crisp and precise look to the masonry.

CHAPTER NINE

THE SURROUNDING DISTRICT

The two towers of Reculver church were added to the building in the twelfth century and were known as the 'Two Sisters'. With various other alterations, this ancient church continued in use into the early nineteenth century when the encroachment of the sea convinced the parishioners that they should build a new church inland at Hillborough. The old church was for the most part demolished, the lead from the towers was sold and the Roman chancel piers were taken away to Canterbury. Salvaged materials were reused in the new church. The towers themselves were, however, a valuable landmark for shipping and were bought in 1810 by Trinity House. They added the wooden vanes, seen in this photograph, to replace the earlier leaded wooden spires, and also took the rather obvious step of building groynes to help protect the rapidly retreating cliffs below their property. The building to the right is the remains of the old vicarage, which had also served as a beer shop – The Hoy and Anchor. This early photograph, sold by F.A. Ridout of 2 William Street, is labelled 'Ramsgate, The Reculvers'.

Opposite: The attractions of the Roman fort and remains of the early church had provided the excuse for visitors to walk along the beach or cliff-top from Herne Bay since the town's earliest days as a holiday destination. In this photograph, taken in the 1920s, we can see that there was little provision made for motor cars. Below the flagstaff to the left of the picture is what appears to be a drag net spread out on the ground to dry.

East Cliffs. This picture shows the cliffs to the west of Bishopstone Glen as they were before being regraded in the late 1960s. The cliffs and slopes behind provided a wonderful playground for local children: cliff slips trapped surface water which provided ponds for newts and frogs, while slow-worms, lizards and rabbits all shared a landscape of long grass and undergrowth that provided cover for camps and dens. In the winter months glutinous clay provided a special delight: hours could be wasted trying to recover lost shoes to avoid difficult explanations at home.

This picture of Reculver dating from the late 1930s or early 1940s shows that car parking had replaced the waving field of corn shown in the picture on the previous page.

The next stage in the story of Reculver is seen here, with caravans covering the fields to the west of the fort and church. Many caravan sites like this provided the opportunity for large numbers of people to enjoy a cheap stay at the seaside, in much the same way as the camp sites around Herne Bay had in the early 1900s (see p. 12).

Beltinge post office in Reculver Road: this photograph was taken by Fred Palmer. The business was run for many years by a Mrs Smith, and this is almost certainly her standing in the shop doorway. The window display is made up of various different picture postcards. Apart from purely local business the shop was handily placed for the many visitors passing through on their way to Reculver; the cliffs between the Downs and Bishopstone were also very popular with walkers. In the years before the motor car became widely available, many people walked or rode bicycles, not just from necessity but as a pleasureable activity. Local guide books from the early 1900s often describe the pleasant walks available in the district, starting out from Herne Bay with routes to the villages of Herne, Chislet, Upstreet or to Reculver. Distance is rarely mentioned unless the round trip was more than about 8 miles.

The Little Brown Teapot could be found in Reculver Road just back from Grange Road. In August 1933, when this picture was taken, the business was owned and run by Mrs Cox. The tea offered at 4½d per cup was 'special', having been made with water softened in a 'Permutit' water softener. The poster to the right is advertising 'Poppies' at the Pier Pavilion; this show was having its second resident season, with the best reserved seats at 2s 6d. If this was too much, unreserved seats (including tax) were 7d.

This small shop built on to the end of a pair of cottages in Canterbury Road just beyond Eddington became a branch post office sometime between 1905 and 1909. The pair of tall houses beyond are Eddington Villas, built in 1896. It is difficult to look at this calm, almost rural scene and appreciate that when the picture was taken this was one of the two main access routes for vehicular transport into the town from the south. The traffic today barely slows down as it passes the spot where the small children are standing.

An aerial view by West of Whitstable, showing the junction of Eddington Lane and Canterbury Road. The large building centre left is Herne Bay College (now Herne Bay Court). The building still stands in its own grounds with only the houses of Parsonage Road to the north before the railway embankment. In the foreground the large house, playing fields and nursery north of Eddington Lane have all disappeared under housing redevelopment since the 1970s. The orchard to the south was redeveloped with bungalows some years earlier.

A handsome set of iron gates dominated the entrance to Strode Park in the early 1900s. This picture was taken by Filmer, a photographer from Faversham who rarely worked this far off his home patch. The line of the wall on the right-hand side of the road still sweeps round into the village much as it did nearly 100 years ago, although the large overhanging trees have long gone. The left-hand side of the road has suffered from some very unsympathetic development. The tree in leaf to the right of the gates in front of the lodge is almost certainly the much trimmed cedar which can still be seen today.

Herne Mill is a smock mill that was built for John Holman of Wingham in 1781. In the 1850s the original three-storey wooden mill was raised on a two-storey brick base. The mill was owned and operated by the Lawrence family until it was sold to the Wootton family in 1879; they continued to operate it as a windmill until 1952 when grinding was done using electrical power. The mill's continued survival owes much to the Herne Society and a large number of volunteers who have raised funds, carried out repairs, and encouraged various public bodies to provide essential funds, ensuring that this important local landmark provides some continuity in an ever-changing Kent landscape.

The village of Herne was a favourite destination for visitors to the area seeking a change from the bustle of the seaside. Walks, cycle rides and charabanc outings all brought visitors to Herne. This picture shows the ancient St Martin's Church. Although the building's walls contain fragments of re-used Romanesque masonry, the church has long been thought to date from the twelfth century. In the 1970s excavations revealed the remains of foundations which could indicate a building of the seventh or eighth century. Documentary evidence is slight but it is perhaps acceptable to think of the foundation of a church at Herne after the devastation of the marauding Vikings. Apart from interest in the ancient church, Herne can also boast its special links with the Reformation of the English Church and its most famous vicar, Nicholas Ridley.

The main road to Canterbury just south of Herne, early 1900s. It has the appearance of a quiet country lane with dappled light filtering through the trees on either side. This is the road that witnessed the area's first motor bus experiments (see p. 104). In the early nineteenth century it had been an important part of the passenger route from London to the Continent, avoiding the sea passage around the North Foreland. The line of iron fencing on the west side, complete with mature trees, has survived until today. The largest trunk, pushing up against the fence, is one of a number of London plane trees. The fields of Home Farm, to the right behind Strode Park, contain many mature parkland trees dating back to the late nineteenth century. This farm has retained field boundaries much as they were 100 years ago, and this important landscape contributes considerably to the setting of the village – which has otherwise been spoiled by almost totally unsympathetic development from every other point of the compass.

ACKNOWLEDGEMENTS

This book would not have been possible without the help of many people. The notes that I originally prepared for *Herne Bay in Old Photographs* were re-read as part of the research for this book and I am grateful to the people who helped me at that time. The publication of old photographs never fails to trigger memories and I am indebted to people who over the years have shared their knowledge of Herne Bay with me. I am particularly grateful to the following individuals and organisations that have freely given me their time and expertise in the preparation of this volume.

British Red Cross, David Bubier, Canterbury and East Kent Postcard Club for the use of their library, M.M. Catt, Mr W.G. 'Nobby' Clark, Dick Eburne, Jack Edwards, Mr S.H. Fry, Manda Gifford, Mr and Mrs H. Gough, *Herne Bay Gazette* office staff, all the staff at Herne Bay Library, Herne Bay Records Society, Debbie Hogben, Trudy Iggulden, Bill Johnson, Max, Jim Newbury, Fred Palmer, Roger Pout, David Ridout, Mr and Mrs R. Root, the Salvation Army, Diane Stingemore, Roy Tassell, Roger Turner.

I apologise to anybody I have inadvertently omitted.

My thanks also go to all the people who for whatever reason have kept old pictures rather than throwing them away; seemingly unimportant photographic snaps make up an invaluable part of the jigsaw of local history.